FORTY IN THE FEMALE LANE

By

PATSY A. MILLS

1stBooks - rev. 2/20/01

BASICS

Truth is all around us. We do not see it because we are in boxes; Some we make for ourselves and some are made for us by other people or circumstances.

Our world is darkness; truth is light.

In our travels, it sometimes happens that our box is breached and we get a glimpse of the light.

It happens unexpectedly and without warning.

It is what we do with these moments of truth that make us or break us and only the one who sees the light may decide what to do with it.

CHAPTER ONE

Nancy Lynn Albers stood with her back to the full-length mirror viewing herself with the hand held mirror. She was thinking about the invitation she had received that morning to her fortieth high school class reunion and remembering that she had "come into her own" in her sophomore year at Portland Valley Central High School.

It was the start of summer vacation before sophomore year and everybody spent most afternoons at the town pool. She had learned to swim at an early age at this pool and was nicknamed "Fish" because of her swimming prowess. She was naturally graceful and athletic, and that year, when she had just turned fifteen, she had developed into a very pretty girl who looked especially good in a bathing suit.

It is difficult to know why those next three summers were so great. She and her friends had little knowledge of the outside world and they were not concerned with larger issues. They spent their days in each other's houses planning parties, going to the pool, hanging out at the local burger joint and trying to figure out what to wear for any event they planned.

Nancy Lynn loved swimming and was usually surrounded by boys who wanted to show off for her. She could out-swim most of them and they spent hours on their technique trying to gain points with her.

In the tradition of fifteen year-olds everywhere in America that summer of 1951, she was passionately in love with a different boy every week or so.

Now, almost forty years later, she looked at herself in the mirror and tried to trace the woman she was now back to the girl of those golden summers She didn't understand how life could have turned out so differently than she had imagined. She had tried to connect her expectations and dreams with some sort of reality, but it was like trying to do a connect-the-dots picture where large sections of the dots were missing.

Sometimes she smiled at her approaching senility and all the tricks she used to remember something from one minute to the, next, but this was different. She had always believed in the promises of those golden summers, but it seemed that life had just kept on going in its frightening, inexplicable way and she had been towed along with the tide. She knew that she had a "real world" self, but on another level, she lived a different, dreamlike, existence. She tried to figure out where she had split off and become two separate persons in one skin.

She put the mirror away and went to stand by the bedroom window to look out at the stand of trees between her house and the neighbor's. She often stood there watching the squirrels and rabbits that played in the area. She had seen deer several times and had formed the habit of speaking softly to the animals when she saw them.

Patsy A. Mills

As she watched the trees, she caught a glimpse of red as the resident cardinal flew past her and lit in the tree closest to the window where she stood.

She had the feeling that her interludes with the stand of trees were, in some way, a connection between the two worlds she lived in. The animals touched her in some deep, primeval way that made her feel real.

CHAPTER TWO

Boots Grayson stood in the hallway looking at the mail. There was an envelope from her hometown with a return address of someone she thought seemed vaguely familiar. She shifted that letter to the bottom of the stack and looked through the rest of the mail. There were the usual circulars, Visa and Master Card offers, bills and a small envelope, which was probably an invitation to a wedding or a graduation.

Most of the women her age had married early and had their families before they were thirty, but their children had waited till they were past thirty to make a commitment to marriage and family. Indeed, many had not married at all and a few had elected to forego marriage and do parenthood alone. Many were nearing forty now and were still working on graduate degrees to lead them to a more fulfilling and financially rewarding life. Boots own two daughters had only recently finished the schooling they had decided they needed and her son was in pediatric residency at a large Boston hospital. Only one of the offspring had married and they had decided not to have children.

Boots had difficulty understanding the different value system of her children. She had been taught that you married and raised a family and that you would be selfless in so doing. There was no mention of a "double standard" when she was growing up and the whole "Consciousness raising" of the seventies was lost on her.

She had married after three years in College and had the children in rapid succession and settled in to raising them and making a home for her husband and children. She was a talented homemaker and she loved being a wife and mother. She had never wished for any other life.

When she lunched or played bridge with her friends, very little was said about discontent or lack of fulfillment. Perhaps they drank a bit too much at lunch or shopped with an unseemly zeal, but there were few conversations where they bared their souls. Mostly, they talked about their children's accomplishments or the latest decorating trend or they detailed the plans for yet another trip or cruise or golf outing. There might have been a certain flatness to their lives but they seemed happy.

Now Boots opened the last envelope to find that a reunion committee from her High School graduating class had been formed and a reunion was set for June, just two months away.

Her first inclination was to toss the invitation into the trash, but she decided to ask Mike if he wanted to go. There had been little contact with her High School classmates over the years. She had gone away to college and then married Mike. IBM had recruited him, and they had moved too far away to visit often when the children were small. By the time the children were old enough to travel,

3

she had lost touch with her classmates. Mike had never been too interested, anyway, in visiting her hometown. Her parents had moved away when her father had been transferred to the Southwest.

She went to the bookshelf where her High School yearbook stood, along with all the other yearbooks from Mike and the children's High School and College days. She leafed through the first few pages of the book and remembered Mr. Askin, their Latin teacher to whom the yearbook had been dedicated that year. Turning the pages, she began to remember the teachers and when she came to the picture of Alma Jackson, her geometry teacher, she stopped, and a wave of nostalgia swept over her.

Boots had loved geometry and Miss Jackson was that rare teacher who loved her subject and her students. She taught with a sureness and competency that was rare in public education. Boots remembered that in Miss Jackson's classes, she had been totally focused on the subject being taught and could see the delicate artistry of numbers and planes. She had seen the world in a different way through the structure of math.

However, even though Miss Jackson loved all her students, she taught to the boys in her classes. The girls were there because math was a requirement for graduation, but the boys were budding engineers, doctors and mechanics and took math with a different purpose in mind. They were, for the most part, interested in college or tech school and had been advised what courses to take to get them into their chosen field. The girls were advised to take home economics and languages and even though Boots loved math, she somehow felt that she needed to concentrate on other areas of her High School curriculum.

She finished all her math classes with top grades and got a pat on the back from her parents and a "well done" from Miss Jackson. There was never any mention that she was especially talented in math or that she might pursue a career other than or in addition to, homemaking.

She never considered any other career, but now looking at the picture of Miss Jackson, she wondered if her beloved teacher had ever thought about encouraging Boots in a career other than homemaking.

She began to think of other classes she had taken in high school and college. She remembered the English and American literature classes where she had read the classics and beautiful poetry and she remembered sitting in the student lounge, drinking black coffee and discussing philosophy.

What had happened to that bright, interested student she had been? Where had she gone in all the years of domesticity? She wondered if all the modern focus on "women having it all" might not have merit.

Mike was going to retire in a few years and she certainly was not needed as a parent any longer and it looked like she would wait a long time to be a grandmother. She must have twenty years more of her life and she knew that bridge, golf and shopping were not going to be enough for the rest of her life. She dreaded Mike's retirement; too, as she was used to having the house to herself and a full dose of her husband did not thrill her. Maybe the reunion would be fun. She could see how everyone else was coping.

CHAPTER THREE

How did I ever lose such complete control of this situation, Sally laughed as she ran after her four year old grandson. He was running, hell bent for leather, for the mall parking lot. Sally had agreed to take care of Patrick and his six-year-old sister, Alicia, while her son and his wife took advantage of a long business/holiday weekend. She had looked forward to having the children and had their room all ready for them so they wouldn't be homesick. However, her grandchildren were not prone to homesickness, they were into moving ahead with life at a much faster pace than Sally could manage.

She had promised to take them to the latest Disney movie and she planned to sleep through the entire thing. She knew they would sit through the movie completely absorbed. They had collected memorabilia about the characters for a month in response to the marketing blitz by the Disney Corporation. She finally corralled Patrick and made her way to the cinema complex where she bought tickets, popcorn and drinks to put in re-sealable cups that she had brought from home. She remembered from past trips that when a child spills a drink at the movies, there's hell to pay all around. The children settled down as the movie began and Sally relaxed into the seat.

She thought about the invitation she had gotten in the morning mail to her high school class reunion. Forty years! She was so glad that someone had gotten all the information and names and made plans for the reunion. It must have been a horrendous job and it would have never occurred to Sally to organize such an event. She was thankful, though, that someone had done it. She had already drafted her acceptance and would mail it Monday.

Sally had always remembered her high school days as a sort of beginning for her. She had been shuttled around without much form or focus when she was young.

Her parents had been killed in a car accident when she was six and it had fallen on her parent's families to provide a place for her and her older brother and younger sister. They had been separated and had lived with different relatives until the particular relative grew tired of the added expense and responsibility. Sally had lived in five different homes by the time she was fifteen.

She was a true testament to her nurture in that she had no focus to her life. She was, however, cheerful and resilient when she ended up at her grandmother's house in Portland Valley at age fifteen. She was scattered, boy crazy and fun to be with.

Her grandmother was an old-fashioned woman with a strong sense of herself and she loved Sally dearly. Sally loved her grandmother, too, but she got away with everything she could. She always figured she could get around any wrath she might incur. However, there was very little wrath. Her grandmother was more prone to long explanations about the importance of manners and why they were important. She believed that there was a proper way to behave for almost all situations. This was news to Sally. No one had ever bothered to impart a social code to her, but because she loved her grandmother, she listened to her. It was difficult to civilize Sally at this point, but inroads were made.

When she landed at Portland Valley Central High School at the beginning of her sophomore year, she was the new kid on the block. Because of all the places she had lived, she was slightly exotic for a small town like Portland Valley. Her grandmother was a pillar of the community, though, so she was well regarded and the other students had no bias against her and liked her right away.

The first day of school, she had gotten into a heated argument with another girl in her class about what "original" meant when it was included on a dress label. Neither of the girls had a clue but each took an opposite tack and fought it out over lunch in the cafeteria. They eventually realized that they were each on shaky ground and gave up the argument.

That was the beginning of a friendship that lasted all the rest of high school. They were fast and true friends and did all those things together that teenage girls did in small, rural towns in America in the early fifties.

They loved drama class, boys, study hall and sneaking cigarettes. They spent hours plotting ways to get in with the popular kids and actually succeeded when they let it be known that they would smoke in the drug store where they hung out after school.

Maxine, (Maxi to everyone) was a townie, having been born and raised in Portland Valley. She had a degree of stability that Sally didn't possess and the two of them made the town their playground. Maxi was already sixteen and was allowed to drive her father's old Chevy sedan circa 1944. She taught Sally how to drive the old floor shift car and, for twenty-five cents, they could buy enough gas to drag all the familiar hangouts and favored boy's houses on Friday and Saturday nights. There were always three or four other girls to pile into the old car.

Sally smiled when she remembered how innocent they were then.

How could they have prepared for the darker side of life that some would have to deal with.

Maybe you don't prepare for it, she mused, and perhaps you just dealt with it when it presents itself. At any rate, she had known the darker side, in spades, and was interested to see what effect life had had on her classmates.

She hadn't kept up with any of them, even Maxine, all having gone off to different areas of interest after high school.

She came out of her reverie as the movie was ending and Alicia and Patrick were begging to go for ice cream.

CHAPTER FOUR

It was very hot in New Mexico where Maxine lived. She had just finished reading the invitation to her high school reunion and thought it not likely that she would travel so far to see people she hadn't seen in nearly forty years. Both her parents had died years ago and her brother and sister had moved away. Most of her classmates had moved on too, and she barely remembered the names of even her friends.

She did remember Sally, however. How could anybody forget a friend like Sally? She had fit all the nooks and crannies of Maxie's personality and they had been inseparable for three years. Maxi often thought that the arrival of Sally in Portland Valley had given her small town life a jump-start. She hadn't thought of Sally for some years and had no idea where she lived now. Sally still had relatives in Portland Valley who might have kept in touch with her, but since Maxi had no ties to her home town, she knew nothing of Sally's whereabouts.

She used to wonder how Sally would have reacted to her sixties counter-culture experience and her latter day born-again Christian experience. There really was a lot she would like to talk over with Sally. Maybe it wouldn't be such a bad idea to go to the reunion.

She thought of her life as it was now; the family and church centered life that balanced her wild side so well-the side that Sally had brought out. She thought of all the boys they had been so crazy about and how each had always told the other who they currently had a crush on before they told any of the others in the group. She wondered how all those boys had turned out and how many would be at the reunion. All the gang would be there too, and it would be exciting to see them. She changed her mind and decided she would definitely go to the reunion.

CHAPTER FIVE

Mary Grace Ghant, Johnson, Hegel received her invitation to the reunion on a day that she was going to New York to accept an award for a film she had produced; a documentary about urban blight and its effect on children.

Mary Grace had long since left her small town life behind and moved into the fast paced life of documentary film producers in New York and abroad. Her social conscience had developed in college where she was lucky enough to study with some of the best minds in American education.

There was never any indication that her professors expected less from their female student than from their male students. This came as a surprise to Mary Grace since she had never worked hard in high school. Fun and games were top priority and no one had expected a great academic career for her. However, she had good grades in high school because she was intelligent .She had applied to an Ivy League college because her current boyfriend planned to go there. He had not been accepted but she had and since her family could afford to send her, she went.

She remembered what a culture shock it had been to enter the academic world of intellect. It took her two semesters to even begin to feel at ease with the importance of ideas. She gradually grew comfortable in the environment and graduated at the top of her class. She went on for a graduate degree in film and had completed her Ph.D. She had been making films and teaching in major universities all over the country. She had had two husbands and was currently single. There was a daughter and a son and four grandchildren.

When she thought of Portland Valley, it was with an eye to the sociological impact of small town rural life on the American reality. She was working on a script on that subject and decided to go to the reunion to do research for her film She was also interested to see the group. They would have much catching up to do as none of them had kept up with the others.

Whoever had made all the arrangements for the reunion was to be commended. It must have been some job and she would never have been able to pull it off. As her mother often said "it takes all kinds to make it all work."

CHAPTER SIX

Nancy Lynn was trying to get through to her daughter, but the line had been busy for hours. Jean was either talking to her friend Susan or she had the phone off the hook so she didn't have to talk to her mother. Nancy Lynn knew that her daughter viewed her daily phone calls as a nuisance, but she still called. She tried to sound cheerful and upbeat when she called, but the irritating neediness always crept into her conversations. She would deviate from cheerful into complaints about her ex-husband, Jeans's father, or her lack of a social life or the cost of keeping up the house.

She didn't have any close friends and hadn't had any for a number of years. Her mother and father were living in a retirement village in Florida. They had a very active life that didn't include her and her other daughter and son lived on the West Coast and rarely called or visited, so she called Jean every day because she desperately needed to connect with someone. Jean didn't want to hear her complaints about Adam and <u>she</u> didn't want to keep harping on the injustices he had inflicted on her, but she felt so betrayed and angry that the subject came up often. The subject had been her primary occupation for the ten years since Adam had walked out on her and told her exactly why he was doing so.

CHAPTER SEVEN

When Nancy Lynn was a little girl and an only child, her parents' world revolved around her. There was enough money to give an only child the things her parents wanted her to have, so that she was somewhat privileged. They lived in the nicest neighborhood and Nancy had clothes bought carefully, lovingly and with a great deal of time invested in their purchase. In addition to swimming lessons, there were ballet and tap lessons, horseback lessons and trips to Disney Land. She was a good little girl, but then, there was no reason not to be good as she was very carefully tended, much like an exotic plant grown in a greenhouse.

After she graduated from high school, she went to college about seventy miles from home. She was excited and happy to be on her own. She and her friends talked of little else their senior year at Portland Valley High.

She didn't have a major or for that matter, a minor so she registered as a Liberal Arts major. A new, appropriate wardrobe was researched through Seventeen Magazine and she and her mother shopped for weeks. There was new luggage and a bank account in her name and anything else her parents' thought she might need

Nancy Lynn had never made a decision all on her own and she had very little input into her college career. She left for college five days before Labor Day in 1953 and by September 15,1953, she was totally miserable. She was lonely and frightened and completely unable to take care of even her new wardrobe. The checkbook baffled her and classes were so unlike high school that she just stopped going. By the first of October, she gave up, called her mother and announced that she was coming home.

Her parents welcomed her and her father gave her a job in his insurance agency. She learned bookkeeping and insurance terminology and lived at home and dated the few men who were still left in Portland Valley.

Eventually, she met one of the clients and they began to date. She felt safe and comfortable with him and he was enamored of her since she was very pretty and flirtatious. They dated for two years, decided they were in love, and got married.

There was a huge church wedding with bridesmaids from her group of friends from high school, who were either already married or graduating from college.

After all the showers and parties and the honeymoon in Miami Beach, Nancy Lynn and Adam settled into the new house that was Nancy's parent's wedding gift to them.

The honeymoon was not an unqualified success. Nancy Lynn was a virgin and would have liked to remain one. Sex was uncomfortable, messy and undignified. Besides, she felt out of her element in Florida and wanted to be back

11

in Portland Valley where she knew every one and could establish a routine that made her feel safe.

However, she liked having Adam take care of her and aside from sex, Nancy Lynn sometimes felt she had never left her parent's home.

One year after they were married, Jean was born. Nancy's parents were thrilled, Adam was thrilled and all attention immediately shifted to the baby. Nancy suffered prolonged postpartum depression and had to be taken away for a two week vacation to recover. Her parents were more than eager to take care of Jean.

Nancy Lynn recovered enough to take charge of her family, albeit, with the help of a live-in maid that her parents paid for.

She developed the habit of spending summer mornings at the pool with Jean and winter mornings were given over to reading romance novels and dreaming of adventures that had nothing to do with her everyday life.

She had few real friends left in Portland Valley by this time. They were scattered all over the country. She was very close to her parents and talked with her mother two or three times a day. Always on Sunday, they had dinner after church at her parent's house. Jean was always dressed in the most expensive little girl clothes available.

All seemed well.

Adam was the epitome of the dutiful husband and father. He had gone to work for his father-in-law shortly after the wedding and even though Mr. Albers' was a hard taskmaster, Adam always made his quotas and he made a very good income. He never considered quitting his job even though he was vaguely discontented. He was far too busy to dwell on any different life. When Jean was three years old, Kevin was born and when Kevin was ten months old, Marcy Lynn was born. Nancy leaned more and more on her parents, but they were tiring of the world of work and the added responsibility of Nancy and her family. One Sunday when Jean was twelve years old, Nancy's parents announced at dinner that they were retiring. They had decided to turn the agency over to Adam and move to Florida. They had obviously been planning this for some time and Nancy Lynn was devastated.

By the year's end, they were in Florida and Nancy was left with a husband burdened with the demands of the agency and three children that she was emotionally ill-equipped to deal with. There was little time for Nancy and Adam to sit down and talk about what they wanted and what was best for the family. Nancy didn't want to talk anyway; she just wanted to be taken care of. Nancy was no better at handling the responsibilities of her family than she had been trying to be a college student. She relied on Adam to make all the decisions for the family. She got them off to school each day as best she could and the maid took care of the house.

For the most part, Nancy spent her days reading and when they got their first television set, she was hooked. She spent hours each day watching soap opera after soap opera. She was emotionally detached from the children. The maid and Adam met their physical needs but very little emotional support came from Nancy.

CHAPTER EIGHT

When Nancy was born, her parents were very careful to make sure no harm came to her. She was watched closely when she played and crossing a street was a major ordeal even when she was ten or eleven. When she started to school, her parents had a list of rules to ensure her safety. Her family was the first to own a car equipped with seat belts. By the time she was twelve, she understood that safety was of paramount importance and it became a part of her life to fear the unexpected danger lurking everywhere.

As she grew into adulthood and was expected to take responsibility for her life, she began to build a protective wall to insulate herself from reality.

When her parents lost interest in protecting her and Adam was too busy, she did what she had to do to survive. She built her dream world and escaped there when she felt threatened. It was difficult to see any other reality when she was enmeshed in her fantasy. There was no family to care for, no husband to connect to and no need to take risks in that world. It become increasingly difficult to get outside the world she had built even though she felt as if she were suffocating . She had no place else to go.....the terror was unmanageable.

She had done well in school. She was not brainy but she was capable and could study for hours when she needed a good grade. Most knowledge that she had picked up in school, though, did not stay with her. She memorized facts and after she had gotten the desired grade, the facts were discarded.

When she was fifteen and had a typical social life, she felt normal. Playing the field in Portland Valley, cruising in Maxie's father's old car and hanging out at the pool were non-threatening activities. She had often wondered if the other girls in the group ever felt afraid. Sally certainly wasn't, nothing seemed to scare her and Maxi, who she had known all her life, never seemed to concern herself with safety. Whenever Nancy gave voice to her fears, they laughed and did whatever they wanted anyway. In the deepest part of her being, she was convinced that they were going to come to a horrible end because they were so careless. She was a sweet and loving friend though, and very popular with the boys, so they tolerated her fearfulness. They had spent hours in her room laughing, talking and making plans.

Funny how she still lived in Portland Valley and they all lived somewhere else. There were nearly forty years separating those days in high school and none of them had yet died from all the terrible things Nancy was sure would happen to them.

She was standing at the bedroom window and a chipmunk skittered into the woods and stopped beneath a tree where he began to dig for some edible treasure. Nancy watched the tiny animal and thought how much a part of the natural world he was. She wondered why she didn't fit in that world any more than she fit in the "real" world. It all boiled down to three worlds really. The fantasy world she had created, the civilized world society had created and that world in microcosm outside her window where the animals and trees lived. She couldn't see the connection, but she had to find a way to be comfortable in her skin so that everything was not so fragmented and frightening.

CHAPTER NINE

Boots had been grocery shopping and was cleaning the produce when Mike came home from work. He looked tired so she fixed him a drink and he sat at the kitchen table while she finished putting the groceries away. She would start dinner when she finished and while it was cooking, she would broach the subject of the reunion.

Mike hated to spend time with people he didn't know but Boots really wanted to go to the reunion. She hoped she could convince him that he would have a good time.

After she had started rice and put chicken in the broiler, she gave him the invitation and told him she would like to go. Mike, as expected, did not want to go and no amount of cajoling changed his mind. Boots had decided she would go even if Mike wouldn't and when she told him her decision, she could see by the set of his jaw that he did not like that idea at all. She thought about backing down and telling him she wouldn't go, but something nagged at her sense of right and she stood firm. They ate dinner in silence and nothing more was said of the reunion. They were going to play bridge with friends and that took care of the rest of the evening.

A week later, Mike called from the office to say he wanted to take some time off so they could plan a trip to see their son in Boston. He had been asking them to visit and see the hospital where he was in residency. When Mike told her the date he was talking about it was the weekend of the reunion. Boots reminded him that she still planned to go and since he would have time off perhaps he would like to go with her. There was a long silence at Mike's end of the line and he finally said that perhaps they could go to Boston another time but he would still pass on the reunion.

He called later in the day to say he would not be home for dinner. He was meeting with some out of town managers and would have dinner with them in town.

Boots knew that Mike would not ordinarily have a dinner meeting, as these meetings were not usually productive, but she knew that he was using the meeting to punish her for the reunion. She was frustrated that they were at an impasse about her decision to go. It seemed at this point, that she should just cancel the trip to keep peace. The second she thought of canceling though, a bell went off in her head. She remembered the picture of Alma Jackson and she remembered that she had been really good in math.

She put the phone back on the hook and went to the refrigerator to see what she could fix for her dinner. She took out lettuce for a salad and went to the sink. As she stood washing the lettuce, she thought about how often in fifty-eight years she had let someone bully her into their way of thinking. As she began to realize the truth of this thought, a wave of pure rage came over her. She realized in amazement that she had been had.

She had been married to Mike for thirty-seven years and had always thought she had a very successful marriage. It occurred to her that the marriage was not so much successful as it was lacking in stress. A stress- free relationship has certain advantages but it is not necessarily a happy marriage. She also realized that the union was stress free because she had always made sure that no one's feelings were ever ruffled. She had made it her job to make everything run smoothly for the family and if that had meant giving in or not having an opinion, and then that was what she did. Mike had made all the major decisions of their marriage with very little input from her. He had decided on the social life they had the houses they had lived in, the children's colleges and even their daily routine was geared around his schedule.

With that bit of late-blooming awareness firmly planted in her brain, she realized she had a predicament. She knew absolutely, in one of those little epiphanies that life hands out every now and then, that she had been dishonest all her life. Following hard on that understanding, she knew that she could never do that again. This revelation was so startling that she was simply floored. She thought back over the years to all the times she had given in; to her parents, her teachers, Mike and yes, even the children. No wonder they were so self-involved. With her as a role model, they had been taught that their opinions and methods were valuable, but hers were not. Her value as a person was questionable and the children had been taught that by her actions.

She had always considered herself a peacemaker, and God knew she had kept the peace, but the peace she had bought was fraudulent and dishonest to herself and her family.

She wondered how she was going to make this right. She knew that Mike would not understand. He would probably think she was crazy. However, Boots had never felt saner or surer of herself.

Her rage had dissipated. She sat in a chair in the family room and thought about what she had discovered. She felt excited and very alive. She could never remember feeling this sense of herself before. It was as if a door had opened and everything came pouring out from the pent-up well of who she was. She had no desire to close that door or to stem the tide of understanding that she was experiencing. She knew that this was the beginning of her real life.

CHAPTER TEN

Cal and Joan had picked up the children and Sally was putting the house back together. She wondered how she had managed to raise a son like Cal. She would have admired him no matter whose son he was.

Cal was the son born to Sally and her first husband, Clarence. As Sally cleaned the kitchen, she gave a prayer of thanks for all the good things that had come of her marriage to Clarence.

They had married when Sally was twenty-three and Clarence was thirty four

She remembered the day they met as though it was yesterday. She had a freshly minted diploma stating that she had met all the requirements for a degree in business.

She had never had a real job and she was on her third interview of the day and it was not going well. She didn't really have any of the qualifications mentioned in the ad and she was not doing very well bluffing.

The interviewer was watching her with a bemused look on his face that Sally read as disinterest. She began to race into an explanation of why she had applied for the job and how quickly she could learn, etc., etc. The more she explained, the less plausible she was. Finally, she just stopped, looked directly at the interviewer and said, "I have no idea what this job entails, I'm as green as they come and I really don't have a clue how quickly I could learn! I've been on two other interviews today and I don't have a clue what they wanted either. However, I did put myself through four years of college in three years with better than passing grades and I'm not afraid to work."

With that, she stopped, sat back in her chair, folded her hands in her lap and waited...and waited. What seemed like five minutes later, her interviewer cleared his throat, started to say something, cleared his throat again and asked, "When can you start?"

The interviewer was Clearance and he told her later that, no way in hell, was he going to let her out of his office without some guarantee that he would see her again. He would have made up a job for her if necessary. He was thirty-one and single and not even remotely interested in a steady relationship. He had dated dozens of women over the years and had made up his mind that he would spend the rest of his life happily single. But his reaction to Sally was immediate and complete. By the end of Sally's first month on the job, it was common knowledge around the office that Clarence was gone, look, line and sinker.

CHAPTER ELEVEN

Sally did prove adept and learned her new job quickly. She advanced and earned frequent raises and began to have a very nice life. She knew that Clarence liked her, but she was not ready to get involved with anyone at this stage of her life. Three years of putting herself through college, working nights as a waitress and studying whenever she could, had left no time for a social life and Sally had promised herself that fun would be a priority after she graduated and got a job.

Her first apartment had two bedrooms, a tiny kitchen, a bath and a living room that she shared with Christine, a friend from college.

She dated several men. Some she had known from college and others she met through friends. She had settled in the same town where she had gone to college and her job was in the business office of a large general contractors firm. She made friends, bought a car and continued to move up in the job. Summer weekends were spent on the water, either on somebody's boat or at the beach. It was always easy to get a car full of friends and co-workers for some sort of fun.

Often as not, Clarence was a part of the group. He liked to be near Sally and tried to find ways to turn her attention his way. He had asked her out several times but she was always busy.

Truth to tell, Sally felt that Clarence was too old for her. She would never tell him that, but she mostly dated men her own age.

Clarence had been brought up to believe that if you wanted something, you could probably have it if you could figure out a way to get it. He really wanted Sally, so he worked on a method to get her.

He observed her at work and play looking for clues. She was fun and carefree, that he knew, but what really made her happy? They had lunch together often but she always paid for her meal. Each Monday, he brought her a red rose for her desk, which seemed to please her. Sometimes he brought her gag gifts and funny cards that made her laugh. He loved her laugh. It was infectious and uninhibited. On her birthday, he set a cupcake with a candle on her desk and had the whole office gather around to sing "Happy Birthday."

Clarence was stymied. He was desperately afraid that Sally would fall in love with someone else while his campaign to win her was going nowhere.

They had been working together for a year when fate stepped in to lend him a hand.

In August, his sister Mary was coming for a visit. He planned a picnic at the lake and invited several people from the office as well as other friends. Every body brought food and Clarence provided the hot dogs and hamburgers. Since Mary had a three-year-old named Chris, he invited families so Chris would have someone to play with.

The day of the picnic was clear and bright as only an August day can be. Clarence obviously loved Chris and played with him in the water and tried to teach him how to play badminton.

Later, while everybody was eating, Mary looked around for Chris. When she didn't see him, she went to the lake and saw Chris about thirty feet out in the water, floundering and going under. There was no one near him and Mary screamed for Clarence. He ran to the edge of the water, spotted Chris and made a shallow dive in. He swam to Chris and brought him back to the shore.

The little boy was not breathing and had turned a ghastly blue color. Clarence quickly turned him over and began artificial respiration on him. By this time, a crowd had gathered around the two of them and Mary was frantic. Clarence worked on his nephew for a full three minutes before Chris began to sputter and gasp. Finally he took a deep breath and began to cry. When he began to cry Clarence picked him up and held him close and he too began to cry in big wrenching sobs. Mary knelt down and took her son and hugged her brother.

Sally was amazed at Clearance's reaction. The whole episode had lasted only five minutes and no one had realized the danger that Chris had been in. Clarence had acted on purest instinct out of love for his nephew and the relief he felt when he realized Chris was shattering.

After a bit, Chris had calmed down and was playing with the other children, being quite the center of attention because of his rescue and Clarence had gone back to tending his guests.

Sally was sitting on a blanket looking out over the lake and playing over in her mind Clarences' rescue of Chris. The look of utter relief and love she had seen on Clearances' face was more revealing of who he was than anything she had seen in the year since she had known him.

She looked to see where he was and saw that he was refilling glasses for some of the guests. She didn't know what she needed to say to him, but she knew she had to tell him somehow, that his love for his nephew had touched her deeply.

She walked over to him and waited while he finished pouring the drinks. When he finished, he looked up and saw her standing there. He saw by her face that a change had taken place in how she perceived him. He put down the glass he was holding and walked to her. She never had to tell him how deeply affected she had been by his love for Chris. He simply put his arms around her and held her. It was just about then that they both knew they were gone......hook, line and sinker.

CHAPTER TWELVE

Maxi was walking to the grocery store and enjoying the beautiful New Mexican landscape. She could see why the area was such a Mecca for artists. She had lived here since 1975 when the commune she had helped start had finally folded. It had been dying for years anyway until finally there was just Maxi and her two kids and Jan and the guy from Germany, Heinz.

After high school, Maxi had opted not to go to college. Her father had given her the old Chevy for a graduation present and she had worked all summer at the local hotel dining room as a waitress. She had saved all her tips and when everybody else went off to college or to work, Maxi took to the open road. The only destination she had in mind was California. She had never been anywhere really and California seemed like the end of the world. She stopped on her way west to visit an aunt and to report back home that all was well. She made her way to Sally's college to say good-bye to her and stayed long enough to meet Jake, who, as it turned out, had always wanted to see California too. He dropped out of college, packed his duffel bag and hopped in the old Chevy. Maxi was glad to have the company and the money Jake would contribute to the expenses.

Neither of them had any job skills beyond waitressing and laborer. Those jobs were easy to find in that late fall of 1953 and Maxi and Jake took as long as they wanted going from town to town, checking out the small mid-western towns so much like Portland Valley. As they went across the Mississippi into Arkansas, they smelled the aroma of pigs throughout the first third of the state. On they went into Kansas, Oklahoma and on to the Grand Canyon, making up their itinerary as they went. They drove the south rim of the Grand Canyon and around to the wilder north rim where they bought beautiful jewelry from the Navaho there.

When Maxi thought back to that drive west, she realized that the interstate highway system was only a dream of the Eisenhower administration. It made her feel like one of the original pioneers to remember that old Chevy on those narrow, twisting roads that went through every town in their path. Roads were for getting to towns then, not for getting around them on the way to somewhere else.

They spent a year on the road just absorbing new experiences.

She smiled when she thought of the two of them so happy to be free. They stopped whenever they liked and went wherever they wanted.

There was very little to fear in 1953-54 on the road in America. The country was free and wealthy and had licked the Germans and the Japanese. It was a very good time to test your wings

Maxi and Jake were the original hippies. They didn't hate the system, though; they just didn't want to be part of it. They were kindred spirits and true knights of the road.

They finally reached California in the late fall of 1954. They had never planned what they would do when they got to California. That was their whole goal......just go to California. Neither had any serious career plans and they weren't old enough or experienced enough to consider this necessary.

The one true love they both shared was the new music that was being heard on the radio. By the time Elvis came on the scene in the mid-fifties they were in the groove. They had settled temporarily in Los Angeles. Maxi worked as a waitress and Jake worked on a construction crew helping build houses for all those young men and women who would produce the children of the baby boom. They lived in a trailer park in East L.A. on the edge of an orange grove. They bought the best sound system they could find.

They stayed together until 1963 and by the time they went their separate ways, they had two children and a collection of several hundred albums of contemporary pop music. They sometimes felt that they had single-handedly discovered Rock and Roll music.

CHAPTER THIRTEEN

The hotel room was on the twentieth floor and Mary Grace had settled in to work on her speech for this evenings award presentation.

She planned to use an old speech, which had been reworked several times, and like an old recipe, she added or subtracted ingredients to suit the occasion. She had the whole day to herself and planned to spend as little time as possible on the speech.

Mary Grace had always felt uncomfortable accepting awards. It seemed so self-aggrandizing to stand up in front of a group of people who knew that anything you do in film requires the talent and labor of so many others. She had sat in the same audiences and watched people accept awards that she knew were earned by many people besides the honoree.

However, the awards gave credibility and generated interest, which resulted in publicity and that, meant wider exposure so she played the game along with everyone else.

She hadn't been to New York in a while and planned to spend the day in the city. She felt a rush of excitement. Anything could happen here.

An hour later, the speech was ready and she was on her way downtown. She had put on jeans and sneakers and planned to walk wherever she went to soak up as much of the city as she could. She was having lunch in a restaurant she had seen reviewed in Gourmet Magazine last month; some sort of Thai/French attitude.

Mary grace's avocation was food. She had started collecting recipes when she was twelve and had boxes and files of recipes she had cut out of magazines or collected from friends and relatives. She had never tried most of them because there was no system to her collection. The point was not to use them anyway. They were more like museum pieces to be visited and looked at and marveled over for their composition and ethnic variety.

Every time she decided to organize the collection she got lost in recipes she had cut out of "Good Housekeeping" or "The Ladies Home Journal" as early as 1948. She had cut out whole pages to get a recipe that had interested her and the snippets of articles, the advertisements and the cooking and food styles never failed to fascinate her.

It seemed that America, settling in to peacetime life after the Second World War, was interested in eating and not necessarily gourmet fare. The recipes tended to "hearty" fare. There was much emphasis placed on meat and potato meals.

She had kept a collection of Gourmet Magazines from her parent's attic circa 1945 that reflected the food rationing and the need to cook with limited resources and she had reread them many times.

CHAPTER FOURTEEN

There had been a five-year lapse between earning her master's degree and her doctorate. It had been a wrenching decision to go back into academia after five years of freedom. Formal education didn't fit Mary Grace's personality. Her elementary and high school years were not conducive to disciplined study. Her undergraduate life was a period of discovery but the study came at great peril to her life style. Going back for another labor-intensive period took many an hour of agonizing decision making.

While she had been an undergraduate, she had met and married Ken. He was a pre-med student who had years and years of intensive study and poverty before him.

They had fallen in love and Mary Grace had gotten pregnant. This was 1956 and unwed pregnancy was verboten, certainly for someone from Portland Valley.

Small town America in the mid fifties was into morality, especially sexual morality, and sex before marriage fell outside the boundaries. That's not to say it wasn't prevalent, you just didn't get caught.

They married just before they graduated. The baby was born in December and Mary Grace began work on her masters while Ken went to work on his medical degree. There was no money to do anything other than pay rent, baby sitting and buy food. They both had borrowed money and Ken had money from the GI Bill of Rights, since he had served in the Korean War. Mary Grace worked part-time as a secretary and Ken tended bar on weekends and during school breaks. They barely passed in the night and neither saw much of their daughter, Lila. She did well, though, and was a cheerful and happy baby.

Under all the work of trying to keep it all together, they still loved each other and Lila. There was just no room in the union for them to grow together. Any growth was a personal growth and they grew away from each other rather than towards each other.

Film and medicine could have been an interesting mix if the careers had already been in place, but the intensity of study and time required to complete their respective degrees totally wrecked the marriage. There was never any question of infidelity or incompatibility, they simply had nothing left for each other.

They divorced after Ken got his MD and Mary Grace had her Masters. He went off to Johns Hopkins for his internship and Mary Grace and Lila went to New York where she began work with a small, independent film company.

Mary Grace learned many things during the next five years, chief among her store of new knowledge; Theory and practice do not come from the same package and love was not what she thought it was.

CHAPTER FIFTEEN

She was eager to get started and put all her education to work. The actual work of putting a film together opened her horizons immensely in that she began to see how all the different areas of film making had to come together to make one seamless whole.

She was able, early on, to visualize a complete work that was still in the planning stages and began to appreciate having talented people in each area of production. She gained a new perspective on people and the real world during her first year in New York.

Creative people are no different than people anywhere. They are ambitious, self centered and political. She learned how petty and devious even very talented people could be and she also learned that working with talented filmmakers was what she wanted to do for the rest of her life. She absolutely loved the medium and ate, slept and dreamed the business. Her first assignment on the job was to do research for a film on the reconstruction of Europe after the Second World War. She spent weeks in the library poring over anything to do with the last five months of the war and into the fifties. There were reams of material and Mary Grace had an impressive file of documentation. The script was to be written from her file and the film would be shot in Europe in the spring and summer of 1959. After the script committee had a look at the size of her file, she was told to weed out as much extraneous material as possible. She spent another month editing and weeding until, finally, it was usable.

The script was finished with Mary Grace sitting on the script committee to assure historical accuracy. After the script was approved, the production crew, which had been in place for weeks, had been working on location sites and getting all legal and technical details worked out. While the physical sites were being secured for filming, Mary Grace compiled a log of footage of the war from newsreels and Hollywood.

During the research process, she had had the assistance of one of the interns on the project; a twenty four-year-old graduate student at NYU named Alex. He found all the reference materials and brought them to her and he helped find the texts she needed. He also collated the data and filed everything chronologically.

He had gone with the location crew to Europe where he had ingratiated himself with the head of production by becoming his lover. He was adept at doing whatever was necessary to get in with anyone of importance who could do anything for him.

When the crew list was completed, Mary Grace found that Alex was chosen to go as script consultant for historical accuracy. She was astonished that he had been asked to go instead of her. He would have to drop out of college for two semesters and he was far from qualified.

She had been with the company less than a year and had nothing to lose by going to the top and demanding that she be allowed to go instead of Alex. She prepared her arguments and met with the production manager. He had all sorts of reasons why he wanted Alex on the project, but the bottom line was that Alex had become too important to him personally and he had boxed himself in with promises to Alex for favors rendered. Mary Grace pointed out that Alex had neither the experience nor knowledge to act as script consultant. The manager acknowledged that, but was locked into his deal with Alex and wouldn't change his mind.

She was frustrated and angry and she could see that logic was not going to win this one for her so she began a campaign to make sure everyone on the crew came to her for assistance on historical accuracy. She made it known that Alex had been an assistant on her research and knew very little about the subject. Eventually, the tide began to turn in her direction. She was the obvious expert and Alex was no more than a gofer.

Just before the crew left for Europe, Mary Grace replaced Alex on the crew.

She was relieved that she had achieved her goal but she worried that she might have made enemies out of people she would be working with down the road, but it seemed she had gained a lot of respect from her co-workers. They had been aware of what was going on and hadn't wanted Alex on the crew but were powerless to do anything about it.

Alex actually apologized to her and asked her to keep him in mind for future projects. "Fat chance" thought Mary Grace. "Your goose is cooked as far as I'm concerned."

She had run into Alex several times over the years. He had ended up in the entertainment industry on the sleazy end starting with "B" movies and sliding downward into soft and later hard core porn. The last she had heard of him, he had AIDS and was not doing well.

CHAPTER SIXTEEN

Lila was almost four when they went to France to film the documentary. She had been raised so far, by a succession of nannies and Mary Grace knew little about how to take care of her. She had made sure Lila was taken care of, but she was away from home while Lila was awake and she actually didn't know the child very well.

She had always assumed responsibility for Lila but had not made any effort to be a loving, traditional mother to her. She would never have faked a loving relationship anyway. She was a very forthright person, not adept at playing games to score points with other people, even if it was her own daughter.

Her first hope was that she could park Lila with her parents while she was in Europe, but they weren't up to such a long commitment. All her efforts to find something to do with her daughter were in vain and she finally decided to take her with her.

After all the passport arrangements, the shots and living arrangements and packing were completed, they boarded the plane to France at Idlewild Airport and headed for Paris. From Paris, they would travel to the South of France and live in a rented cottage for the duration of the filming.

Lila was a quiet child, not out of shyness, but because she was intelligent and observant. She asked her mother questions about everything and Mary Grace absent-mindedly answered her. After they were settled on the plane and Mary Grace was not so distracted, she began to answer Lila's questions much as she would an adult, having had little experience talking to children. If she saw that Lila didn't understand, she searched for ways to explain her answer. She didn't know how to talk down to anyone and she didn't talk down to Lila. Lila had never had a really intelligent person take her seriously and even though she was very young, she responded to Mary Grace.

Her manners were decent, as Mary Grace had insisted that she have nannies and sitters with good credentials who would teach her civility and good habits. She was very bright which was no surprise, due to her parents, and she took full advantage of her mother's attention.

By the time they were in Paris, they were comfortable with each other. The pressure of the last year was off and they had a week before Mary Grace was to report to work. They found their cottage and moved in.

The place was furnished even to linens and was clean and cozy. Mary Grace had never been to Europe and her French was not great, but she felt at home immediately. The cottage was on the outskirts of the village, a short walk from the bakery, the butcher and the weekly farmers market.

Everyone seemed to ride bikes, so she decided to buy one for herself and try to teach Lila how to ride also. She found an ancient one for herself with pedal brakes and no gears. There was a basket on the front and panniers on the back for shopping and picnics and touring the countryside. Lila's bike was brand new and bright yellow.

Mary Grace tried to remember when she had learned to ride her first bike and decided she had been about five. It seemed like she had always known how to ride a bike and didn't think Lila would have a problem. Wrong! They spent a good part of that first week in the road in front of the cottage learning to ride the yellow bike.

Lila liked the idea of riding the bike and worked doggedly to keep the thing upright. She fell so many times that her knees wore scabs for weeks afterward. Mary Grace absolutely loved teaching her and by now the pattern had been set that Lila looked to her mother for answers and Mary Grace found the best answer and stayed with her daughter until she understood.

By the end of the week, Lila could ride the bike and Mary Grace had fallen in love with her daughter.

When Lila had been born, Mary Grace had spent three days in the hospital, champing at the bit, to get back to work on her masters. There was none of that mystical bonding that is supposed to take place between a new parent and their baby. She took responsibility for Lila as did Ken but neither of them had any time to be with her.

Ken had not seen his daughter more than three times since the divorce, the last time being when he came to New York to see them off to France. That meeting had been strained. Lila and Ken were complete strangers and Mary Grace and Ken were so wrapped up in their own lives that they would have been better off to have skipped the whole visit.

Now, in their little cottage in France, Mary Grace realized that everything that was important to her was related to this new love she felt for Lila.

They were bonded now in a new relationship so natural and complete that it was weeks later before Mary Grace realized what had happened.

She was standing at the kitchen sink cleaning wonderful, fresh tomatoes, plump eggplants and leeks.

As she worked to get sand out of the leeks, she glanced up to see Lila playing in the back yard. The afternoon sun bathed the yard in a golden glow. Lila was sitting in the grass trying to make a clover chain and Mary Grace was pleased to see her working so hard on her project. When she looked up again, she saw her daughter sitting in the grass with the sun on her shiny dark curls. Mary Grace caught her breath at the simple beauty she saw. She had never seen so perfectly revealed what true art was all about.

She stood at the sink watching Lila with tears running down her cheeks. Lila looked up and saw her there. She smiled at her mother and went back to her project. The moment passed but a door had been opened in Mary Grace's heart that would give her a focus and a direction for her work and her life.

CHAPTER SEVENTEEN

Willard Scott was telling America all about the beautiful people who were turning 100 on the "Today Show". The weather report for the nation looked good and the local forecast was for clear and sunny with a high of 75 degrees and a low of 60.

Nancy Lynn was watching TV in the kitchen as she fixed toast and coffee for breakfast. She looked out the window and saw the sunny sky. She thought, "How odd that the weather is the same here in Portland Valley as it is on television." Then she realized that of course the weather was the same, it was a local forecast that she had just seen.

It was hard for her to separate fact from fiction and since the television was the purveyor of fiction and helped her build and support her own fictional kingdom; she had trouble separating the two worlds. She took her breakfast to the screened porch to eat and the phone rang just as she was sitting down. She was startled since she got very few calls and never any at 7:30 A.M. She went to the kitchen to answer the phone. The caller was Sally and it was a moment before Nancy Lynn realized who she was. Once she understood who was calling, she was overjoyed and asked, "Sally, how are you?" She was so glad to hear her voice and she was bubbling over with excitement.

She asked Sally if she was coming to the reunion and Sally said that was why she had called. She had called Glen, the reunion organizer, for Nancy's phone number so they could plan a get -together of their own before the reunion. She asked if Nancy Lynn knew whether Maxi, Mary Grace and Boots were coming. Nancy Lynn didn't know but promised to call Glen to see how many responses he had gotten. She asked Sally where she planned to stay in Portland Valley and since Sally had not made arrangements yet, Nancy invited her to stay with her. She had a large house and no one but she lived there. She still had a cleaning lady twice a week so she would love to have Sally. Sally accepted her invitation and told Nancy she would call later in the week with details of her arrival and to see who was coming to the reunion.

After she had hung up the phone, Nancy Lynn went to get her invitation for Glenn's phone number. He lived on the outskirts of Portland Valley on the other side of town and Sally didn't see much of him and his wife. They both belonged to the same church, but Nancy was an infrequent attendee. She looked at the clock and saw that it was just before eight and decided it was not too early to call. Glen's wife, Margaret, answered and Nancy Lynn told her she had just heard from Sally and Sally wanted to know if Maxi, Mary Grace and Boots were coming to the reunion.

She and Margaret chatted for a bit about the reunion and Margaret asked how she was doing. Nancy started to say something about how lonely she was and how angry she was with Adam when she realized that Margaret probably didn't want to hear all her troubles. Instead, she surprised herself and said she was fine and really looking forward to the reunion. She asked Margaret how she was and really listened as Margaret told her about Glen's expected retirement and how all three of their children were married and lived out of state. Nancy Lynn commiserated with her about having children too far away to see very often.

After she had gotten the phone numbers for Maxi, Mary Grace and Boots, she offered to help with the reunion if she was needed. Margaret thanked her and said she would get in touch, as there was lots of work to be done yet. After the phone call, Nancy Lynn started a list of things to do. She decided to invite the entire group to stay with her since she had plenty of room. She couldn't call Maxi in New Mexico as it was still too early. She put in a call to Mary Grace and got her answering machine. She left a "voice from the past" message on the machine and asked her to call about the reunion and invited her to stay at her house. She told her she had already talked to Sally and she would be there.

Next she called Boots and she answered the phone. Nancy Lynn told her who she was and Boots was so surprised and glad to hear from her old friend. They talked and laughed for fifteen minutes about how many wrinkles they each had and how many pounds they would have to lose before the reunion.

Boots said that she would probably be coming alone, as Mike didn't want to come. She would let Nancy know at least a week before the reunion. They said good-bye and Nancy Lynn went back to her very cold breakfast.

As she ate her toast, the cardinal flew by with a load of nest building material in its beak. Nancy called to the cardinal and said "Hey bird! I'm going to have company. My friends are coming to Portland Valley and we are going to have so much fun. I can't wait to see them and I think they are glad to be coming to Portland Valley. "

She laughed at herself and how alive she felt. It was a beautiful morning and the world was in an explosion of growth and newness. She felt wonderful and she hoped Margaret did call her with a job to do on the reunion. She was beginning to remember so much about the class and she thought she would like to help plan whatever entertainment there would be.

She called Maxi at noon and Maxi was delighted at the prospect of staying at Nancy's with their friends. It would be like old times.

Later in the afternoon, Jean called and when Nancy answered the phone, Jean asked her if she was all right. Nancy said "of course I am, why do you ask?" Jean told her that she had missed her call in the morning and she was concerned about her. Nancy was touched. She knew Jean didn't look forward to her morning calls but she was worried when her mother didn't call. She told Jean that she appreciated her caring. She told her about the reunion and having all her friends stay with her while they were in town.

Jean had never heard her mother so excited and involved with anything outside of her own pain. She liked the change and offered to help her mother get ready for her house party. That seemed like a very good idea to Nancy Lynn and she would get together with her to make a list of all she wanted to get done.

She decided to go for a walk because it had turned out to be a perfect day.

She stood by the window in her bedroom while she put on a sweatshirt and pants. She saw the bleeding hearts that had just begun to bloom and she felt as if her brain were dancing. She didn't know if she was having a caffeine high or if it was still possible to feel this good. She really didn't care where this feeling of joy was coming from; she welcomed it with an open heart.

CHAPTER EIGHTEEN

When Mike came home from his dinner with the out of town managers, Boots was still sitting in the family room. She had been there all evening, failing even to eat the salad she had started to prepare for herself. Her mind had been racing for hours and all her energy had gone to sorting out the thoughts that were coming to her. With no attempt to guard her feelings or control her thoughts, freedom reigned!

After fifty-eight years of controlling her every thought and emotion, she had stopped, cold turkey!

When Boots was a little girl, her older sister had read fairy stories to her. Boots could never get enough and when she learned to read, she read the stories to herself. She had loved "Cinderella" and "Sleeping Beauty." All the stories had a pattern and they all ended happily ever after. They made a big impression on a little girl who loved order and beauty.

Its fair to say that Boots developed the "Cinderella Syndrome" early in life when it would become a part of her permanent psyche, much like the indoctrination of children by religious organizations.

As she progressed through her early years, she continued to believe that love and marriage automatically brought ever-after happiness. She was reinforced in this belief by her upbringing. If you aim for marriage and children, each succeeding event would make life become more and more perfect.

She never had any reason to doubt this, as hers was a reasonably happy home. Her mother was a good homemaker and mother and was always there for her children. Her life was her family and the family accepted that role for her without question. She never complained and if she was unhappy with her role, nobody ever knew.

When Boot's mother had married in 1919, men worked hard in their world and women worked equally hard in their world and this was the norm across the broadest spectrum of American culture.

They really weren't "happy ever after," but they worked too hard to worry about it. The ideals and attitudes that developed over many years, out of the need for the society to grow, promoted two distinct cultures, one male and one female. This division had shown up in most cultures over the thousands of years of human cultural evolution.

By the early 1900's, the schism produced people who could not relate spiritually or intellectually and even though they shared a common language, the nuances of each was lost on the other. It was similar to two countries agreeing to coexist for the common good. This was accomplished by stringent rules of behavior for each cultural entity and those who dared step outside the boundaries were reprimanded.

The natural physical attraction of the sexes was dealt with by providing the liaison of male and female, but was governed by very strict rules of conduct so that neither camp suffered any loss of autonomy.

With the subsequent lack of real social intercourse, the sexual attraction mutated.

When two people are forced to live together for structure and propriety and have no idea who they are living with, numbness and confusion flourish. Children born in the middle of the great depression were the beneficiaries of this abnormal growth.

The country had grown and flourished. Great expanses of land had been conquered and tamed and there was happiness just around the bend everywhere. At least as soon as Roosevelt could fix the depression or the men could turn over one more patch of dirt for crops.

The women worked to make the dream come true too. They kept everything together on the home front. Everybody worked, including the children and most everyone was enamored of the dream and were convinced that the satisfaction of hard work and a job well done was sufficient reason to get up everyday.

There was also the very real necessity to keep the proverbial wolf away from the door. The whole of American culture supported the dream. The schools taught it, the churches preached it and the beginnings of the advertising industry used it to sell merchandise.

All the hard work brought forth growth in agriculture and technology and the world was opening up. People in Tennessee were privy to the same information as those in California via newsreels and radio. Travel became easier and easier and people migrated all over the country breaking down regional cultural differences. Businesses were going international and this fueled changes in other lands.

Wars came and went, but business drove inexorably into the hinterlands of the world. Roads were built into jungles and hi-rises grew in Africa. As the world opened up and became less of a mystery, people were seeing, up close and personal, how other cultures operated.

As each new technology came on the market, the culture in America shifted and reshifted. What America had deemed the foundation of their being began to crumble. Women had moved into the work place and began to question the value of marriage as they had known it.

Men had carved out a more comfortable place for themselves in the culture and were amazed when women began to challenge the existing order. The order was changing, needed to change and they didn't want to admit it.

Boots and her generation of women were born at the right time to enter the old culture but would be smack in the middle of the new wave, just about the time they would be sure that all their dreams were going to come true someday.

Boots hadn't thought all this through, but she had a glimmer of knowledge that burned dimly on the horizon and she was working her way in that direction when Mike came home. She was barely aware that he had come home and when he came into the family room and spoke to her, she jumped. The house had been quiet for hours and she had been lost in thought.

When she saw him there, she didn't immediately recognize him.

Mike had stayed late after dinner. There had been old friends from out of town to catch up with. IBM had been a world unto themselves for years and management could go to any installation in the world and meet the same people over and over. They spent hours talking IBM-ese and they enjoyed their business relationships even if there was little social significance. These were men and later women who had made their jobs their life and they supported each other in the quest to affirm their decisions.

Mike had had two martinis after dinner and was feeling pleasantly buzzed and amorous. He had decided that he would go home, make love to Boots and then resolve the issue of her high school reunion. He did not like the idea of her going to the reunion alone. He couldn't say exactly why, but it had made him uncomfortable from the first time she had mentioned that she would go without him.

When he came into the house from the garage, he saw a light on in the family room. When he walked into the room, he saw Boots in the chair and thought she had fallen asleep. A wave of tenderness swept over him and he walked over to wake her up with a kiss. He saw that she was awake and saw her jump when she realized he was there. He was discomfited since he had already played out the scenario in his mind as to how the evening would progress. He did give her a kiss, but the combination of the martinis and the garlicky dinner had left him with bad breath. Boots would ordinarily have accepted his caress and made no mention of the bad breath. She had long ago realized that she couldn't pick on him for things that were transitory. However, the combination of the bad breath and her venture into unexplored worlds of thought left her without her usual control and she winced when he kissed her. He saw the look on her face and drew back in surprise and the beginnings of hurt feelings.

He turned away from her to go into the kitchen for a drink of water. Boots didn't follow him into the kitchen, as she would have done ordinarily. She decided that if he wanted something, he could get it for himself. She had reached the point in her thought process where she realized that she couldn't undo anything she had done in her life. If she had been wrong and dishonest, she had been what she had been raised to be. What she had been was not going to change. Change belonged to now and the future.

CHAPTER NINETEEN

Mike came back to the family room slightly chastened, trying to sort out a new tack for handling the reunion matter with Boots. He felt they must get it resolved as it was causing too much tension.

He was used to having Boots defer to him when he really put his foot down but he didn't want to go that route. He would handle it like a problem at work; he would use logic. He didn't realize that this was not a logic problem. He set great store in logic and he was pretty sure he could show her the error of her decision.

When he asked her how her evening had gone, she was almost dreamy and distant in her reply that she had spent the evening thinking.

He looked at her more closely and felt there was some subtle change in her face. She sat in the chair not doing anything. No TV, no needlework and no novel by the chair. He had never known her to give in to long periods of introspection. She was always busy at something. After the children had left home, she had branched out into volunteer and church work in addition to golf and bridge and lunch with her friends.

His first thought was that she might not feel well, but no, she said she felt fine. He asked her what she had been thinking about for three hours and smiled at the thought of Boots keeping her mind on any subject for more than five minutes. She was a doer not a thinker. It was hard for Boots to articulate what had happened to her. She knew Mike couldn't grasp such a drastic change in her new perception of herself and she knew she would have to deal with that, but she had so much yet to sort out.

She told him that she had been going over her life and trying to make decisions for the rest of her life. She hadn't come up with anything significant yet, but she was trying to make some sort of change.

He wasn't at all sure what she was talking about and he instinctively knew that now was not the time to bring up the reunion. He decided to go to bed and asked if she was coming to bed. She would be up shortly, she said.

Mike felt her separation from him but was powerless to do anything about it. He went to the bedroom and showered. He hoped she would come to bed soon as he was totally sober now and wanted her in bed to comfort him, not to make love to.

Boots stayed in the chair the rest of the night, drifting off to sleep and waking up to resume her thoughts. She was not aware of anything else in the house. She was totally captured by the process of thought that her self-allowed freedom was giving life to.

She went to the kitchen at six a.m. to make coffee. Mike came down as soon as he smelled it. He asked her where she had slept and she told him that she hadn't slept very much, that she had spent the night in the chair. This was aberrant behavior for Boots and he asked her to tell him what the problem was.

He thought perhaps she was angry because he wouldn't go to her silly reunion with her. He asked her if that was the problem and she told him that the reunion was no longer an issue. She told him that Nancy Lynn had called and invited her to stay with her and that her group of friends from high school would also be staying with Nancy and that he was not expected.

Mike was a bit put out by this turn of events. He had expected to talk Boots out of going and to find that she was going and didn't even want him to go was a bit galling. He was floundering around in his brain trying to find the logic in this new Boots.

He had pretty much figured out what made his life work and his control of his family was a very important part of his success. To have Boots make plans and go forward with them without any input from him was outside the boundaries. There was no logical explanation for any of this! He was stymied and didn't know what to say.

Mike never jumped into a situation in panic or anger. He always thought everything through and decided he had better give this situation some thought.

He was beginning to feel like Boots was a stranger and he was on the outside trying to get inside and beginning to feel a bit desperate. The lack of her usual self-control had rendered Boots into a mysterious person of some imperceivable power that Mike couldn't grasp or define. He decided to go to work. He could deal with the world of IBM where things fit a pattern and logic applied, solved all problems.

CHAPTER TWENTY

Sally was shopping for clothes to take to the reunion. The trip back home was taking on a life of its' own.

After she had talked to Nancy Lynn and accepted her invitation to stay with her, she had called an elderly aunt who still lived in Portland Valley.

Her aunt was so glad that Sally was coming home and wanted her to stay with her. The aunt was eighty-four and her husband was eighty-nine. He was confined to a wheelchair due to a stroke several years ago. Sally told her aunt that she was staying with Nancy but that she wanted to visit and take them out to dinner. Her aunt knew of several restaurants that were handicapped accessible.

That settled, Sally began to work out the logistics of the trip. She had already told her partner that she would be away for a week. Business had been slow anyway.

Sally had owned her own business for twenty years and had recently taken on a partner in the hopes of slowing down and possibly retiring by the time she was sixty-five. If things went as planned, she would be able to sell the business to her partner for a tidy sum and with her investments and savings and the sale of the business she would make a tidy profit.

CHAPTER TWENTY ONE

She had started out in real estate working for a local broker, but when they were bought out by a national chain of Realtors the business changed for the worse and Sally decided to start her own catering business.

With the assistance of Cal, who was just out of college, she worked out the blueprint for the business, dug into her savings and bought a caterer's truck. She remodeled her kitchen at home into a commercial kitchen and went to work.

The first two years were tough, but with advertising, word of mouth, innovative party planning, and hard, hard work, the business had grown.

Sally was very proud of her business. It had helped bring her back from despair after Clarence had died.

Even now, when she thought about that time in her life, she shuttered to think how close she had come to losing it.

After they were married in 1958, they had taken a new, larger apartment near work. By their first anniversary, Sally was pregnant with Cal, and she had stayed home to take care of him after he was born.

Before too much time had passed, they bought an old Victorian home in the older section of town that had once been the elite section. They remodeled and added a bathroom and a large playroom because she was pregnant again. After Jimmy was born, there was another little surprise two years later in the form of Kari.

Clarence was a real asset to the contracting firm and was eventually made vice president with the firm's intention of making him CEO by the time he was fifty. He was totally in love with Sally and his children and Sally loved him more than she had ever dared to hope. There were no false barriers between them and no hidden agendas to impede the growth of their union.

Both wanted their children to have the opportunity to be everything they could be and organized their lives around that goal.

They understood early on, that if they were going to spend the rest of their lives together, they would have to work on the relationship every day. They shared the responsibilities of the children because Clarence didn't want to miss any of their growing up years. The love that Sally had seen him exhibit for his nephew, Chris, was even deeper and purer for his own children.

He was involved in all aspects of their lives. The other mothers laughed when he brought Kari to her dance classes and struggled with her to get her ballet shoes on. He sat and watched her dance and marveled at her beauty and grace. Whether she was actually beautiful and graceful was not important. To Clarence, who was besotted with her, she was perfect.

Sally took evening classes in whatever interested her at the moment. The local community college and the high school offered continuing education classes in all sorts of fields. She took sewing classes, cooking classes, bridge and golf classes and an art class and as a result, she was a jack of all trades and master of none. However, she was pretty good at most everything she tried so she kept on taking classes.

Clarence liked to hear her excitement when she was learning something new. She would get totally involved in a project

Due to her latest class, her family was either the beneficiary or the victim of her learning, depending on how good her teacher was or how far along in the class she was.

They bought a weekend home at the lake and taught the children to swim as early as possible. Mary and her husband and Chris lived close enough to visit often and the cousins got along well.

Even though she had not grown up with her own sister and brother, they had developed a close relationship once all had married and had children.

Since Sally was generally upbeat and Clarence was happier than he had ever been in his life, nothing prepared them for the Saturday morning when Sally was thirty-four and Clarence was forty-five.

Clarence had taken Jimmy and Kari to their various Saturday morning activities. He had to pick up one other boy on Jimmy's little league team and drop them off at the game and then deliver Kari to a friends' house for an overnight. After that, he would go back to the game and stay until it was over.

It was ten in the morning and it was a beautiful day. Sally and Cal were in the back yard cleaning up the area where Clarence had built a massive, homely barbecue pit that Sally loved. There was construction material strewn about and Sally and Cal were determined to set the area right and cook steaks for dinner.

The phone rang at 10:30 and Cal went to answer it. He came to the back door and yelled to Sally that the phone was for her.

A man asked if she was Mrs.Clarence Caldwell, and when she had identified herself, he told her that he was calling from the hospital and that her husband had been in an accident. He asked if she could come to the hospital. He had no other information for her except that he was from the local police force.

She called to Cal and told him that Dad had been in an accident and that they had to go to the hospital. On the way to the hospital, she prayed over and over in silent desperation that Clarence was all right and that none of the children had been with him. She wasn't even sure that the accident had been a car accident. The policeman had only said there had been an accident.

"Please God, Please God" she prayed over and over. When she got to the hospital and told the receptionist who she was, there was an immediate reaction. A doctor was paged and a nurse who stayed with them took her and Cal to a waiting room. She asked what had happened but the nurse only said to wait for the doctor. He would be here soon.

By the time the doctor got there, Sally was very sure that something awful had happened.

The doctor told her that a young woman had run a stop sign at high speed and hit Clarence's car broadside on the driver's side. Clarence was killed on impact and Jimmy and his friend had died in the ambulance on the way in to the hospital. Kari was still alive but in critical condition. Sally gave the phone number of the parents of the other little boy. They took her to identify Clarence and Jimmy. Kari was still in surgery and would be for some time, but the doctor cautioned Sally that she was in very bad shape and not expected to make it. She died on the operating table and the Doctor came to tell Sally and Cal that they were not able to save her. She asked the Doctor to find someone to help her, as she didn't know how to make any arrangements. That had not been one of the classes she had taken.

After she had begun the preliminary steps, she and Cal drove home.

It was twelve thirty in the afternoon. How quickly her life had gone from her.

When they got home, Cal sat with her in the back yard until Jimmy's friend's mother called. Sally was beginning to settle into numbness. She called Mary and her sister and brother and she called the president of Clarence's company. She never heard their words of shock and sadness, their expressions of sympathy. She just reported the event and went on to the next person on her list.

The funerals came and went and friends and relatives brought food and company and Sally felt nothing. She was in a profound emotional shock and Cal was the only person she could deal with. He had been so strong for her and was always there when she called him. He understood without being told that his mother loved him but that she was deep and far away from herself. He was in somewhat of a shock himself but he was young and resilient.

He carried the burden of his mother's grief all that summer. He never complained that his life had suddenly stopped too. He just stood by his mother.

In September, when school started and he was ten, he went into forth grade with a new maturity and an aura of quiet strength about him.

He had grieved alone for his father and brother and sister. He dreamed often that they were still alive. Dreams he would wake up from and realize he had been dreaming. He would lie in bed and sob silently for his loss. By summer's end, he had begun to play with his friends and picked up his young life where he had left it when it had been so awfully interrupted.

CHAPTER TWENTY TWO

Sally was emotionally numb all that summer. She was not able to grieve or even think about what had happened. She got up each morning and did what was necessary to keep herself and Calvin fed and clothed.

After Clarence's will and life insurance had been settled, she set up her funds in annuities and stocks. Clarence had had considerable life insurance and she would be able to keep the house and have enough money to provide for herself and Cal for a long time, so there was no need for her to go to work.

Perhaps if she had been forced to go out and work, she could have recovered earlier, but she was not able to concentrate on anything for very long.

She dreamed too, at night that Clarence and the children would come to her and all would be as before. When she woke up, she would have to face again that they were gone. She could not say" gone forever." That was too harsh and unrelenting

Eventually, sometime in that fall, she grew angry at the injustice that had fallen to her lot. She had lost her parents in a horrible auto accident and now, her family. She was in a rage at God and took to screaming at the sky and berating God for all the hurt he had allowed to come into her life. All the pain of growing up unloved and unwanted surfaced. She was enraged at Clarence for leaving her. There seemed to be no end to her anger and bitterness. She went through so many phases of grief that she was emotionally unraveled and empty after a while. Her family and friends could see the terrible pain she was in but nobody could reach her. She finally reached rock bottom and had no resources left and she contemplated suicide daily.

And then a small miracle happened.

Much like her love for Clarence had been revealed to her through his love for Chris, Cal was the instrument of Sallys' healing. He was in fifth grade at the time. He was a good student and he had a growing range of interests. Mary's husband had taken him under his wing as well as one of the other fathers in the neighborhood. They had helped him complete work for his Boy Scout badges and had taken him to hockey games and other ball games. He had many friends at school and in the neighborhood and he was a very easy kid to be with. He reminded many of Sally's former personality and sense of fun.

He had talked Sally into letting him keep a disreputable mongrel that had followed him home from school one day. Sally suspected that feeding the dog all the way home had been the inducement for the dog's love and loyalty. However, Sally gave her permission and they scrubbed him and named him George. He didn't clean up very well but he was very much at home with Cal and Sally. Cal poured all his pent up love and hurt into that dog.

George slept with him and sensed when he was troubled or sad. He ran joyfully after sticks that Cal threw for him and ate anything that wasn't nailed down.

Sally came into the kitchen one afternoon and spotted Cal and George on the back porch. Cal hadn't heard her and she realized that he was reading to George. The dog sat next to Cal with his scruffy ears all perked up and appeared to be absorbing the story that Cal was reading. The scene was so comical that Sally started to laugh. She ran from the kitchen so that Cal wouldn't realize that she had seen him. She made it to the living room before she collapsed in hysterical laughter. She laughed and laughed and could not stop. Every time she thought of George getting educated, she would start again.

Eventually she laughed until she started to cry. As soon as the floodgates were opened, she cried as hard as she had laughed. She cried out all the anger, the hurt and the loneliness.

By the time she had stopped crying, she had begun to realize that life was good and Cal was the living proof of that. She figured that she would get back into life and make Cal one very happy little boy. She would make sure that he knew that his life was very important to her and that he was exquisitely loved.

CHAPTER TWENTY THREE

Maxi had left East L.A. when she and Jake had broken up. He went off to San Francisco to check out Haight Ashbury. He was interested in the drug scene and Maxi was not at all interested in drugs. She was still Portland Valley material, just a mite more free.

She hadn't deliberately tried to join the hippie movement in their drifting from place to place. She was too old in the first place and she thought they were pretty inane. Too many "groovys" got on a person's nerves.

She got caught up in the movement because she was a drifter herself. She was disaffected with traditional society and did not want to be a part of it. She identified with the need to break out. She had been raised in the same environment as they had and felt the need to be rid of convention.

Loathing of convention had started when she was a teenager and could see the proverbial "hand writing on the wall." She could never see herself in a hot kitchen, surrounded by several screaming children. The mere image had made her shudder.

She realized that there might be other options, but she was no fighter and trying to do something unconventional in a conventional society was not for her. She had taken the only way she felt was open to her. She left convention behind and went on her own way

Maxi had found it interesting that she had found a subculture anywhere she went at any level she was at. In L.A., In the trailer park, she and Jake had formed friendships with people who were on the lower end of the scale and who, for the most part, didn't give a shit. They all drank beer or cheap wine, hung out together in the small yards of the park and listened incessantly to loud rock and roll pumped out through someone's trailer window. There were illicit trysts, loud arguments, loving fathers and mothers and children who could grow up to be president of the United States.

When they left the trailer park, everybody knew that Jake and Maxi were splitting up, but they threw a huge farewell party for them anyway. It was a blast.

Maxi kept in touch with Jake through the grapevine of drifters. He stayed in San Francisco for a year and drifted north with a group of bearded men and long-haired girls in beads and vests.

Looking back now, Maxi realized how conventional they had been. Back then though, they were the new wave and not too bashful about it.

Jake had kept a diary of his travels. As he wrote day by day, he knew that some day he would chronicle the events of those years.

By the time he was thirty, he had already been through his drug and drifting phase and had settled by the Pacific in Carmel and was writing "The Great American Novel." His first two books were published and not very successful but by the time he wrote his third book about those people who were known as "Hippies", he knew what he was doing. He created a cast of characters with so much humor and love that the whole world seemed to identify with them. He made a fortune from the book and the subsequent movie. He was truly overwhelmed by his sudden success. He dropped out again, hid in Maxie's commune for two years and continued to write.

CHAPTER TWENTY FOUR

By the time Maxi was twenty-eight, she had two children, a boy and a girl. Jake was their father. He loved the children but was in no way committed to raising them.

Motherhood had come a lot more naturally to Maxi than she would have thought. Her parenting was decidedly unconventional, but all the youngsters born into the hippie movement of the sixties got the same type of parenting, so they felt secure and indifferent to their lot.

She was raising the children and working forty hours a week as a tour guide in a winery in Northern California. She was living with her current "old man" in a large, ramshackle farmhouse rented to them by the owner of the vineyard. There were six adults and five children, none of them a product of a legal marriage. They shared their money and the workload and everybody did what they did best. Food was prepared by one of the men who loved to cook. He was also responsible for growing the vegetables they ate. Maxie's specialty was organization and she kept the books, paid the bills and kept everybody going in the right direction at the right time. Nobody was thrilled with cleaning and laundry, so those chores were done on a haphazard basis. There was always a struggle to find anything decent to wear each day to work.

One of the men was working in construction and had heard about jobs available in New Mexico working on the interstate highway system.

Kurt, who was Maxie's mate, and John, broached the idea of moving to New Mexico to start a commune with an open door policy. They would allow anybody who needed a place, to stay for whatever time they required. The idea appealed to everybody and they packed up their few belongings, which included a huge collection of rock and roll and folk albums and their sound system.

They actually had the requisite VW camper/bus with the carryall rack on top. Maxi was still driving the '44 Chevy from high school which was well rusted by now but kept in running condition by Kurt who was a mechanic.

They arrived in New Mexico on a Monday and by Wednesday all three men had jobs on the construction crews.

Maxi and the other two women, Mary and Gail, went looking for a piece of land They found a four acre site two miles outside of town and made an offer to buy it. Their price was accepted and they were joint owners of the plot of land.

They would build the commune according to their own plans and do most of the work themselves.

Maxi ordered every construction book and free pamphlet from the "Whole Earth Catalogue." In the meantime, they lived in the VW and two large tents.

The first order of business was water and they hired a well digger who struck water the second day of drilling. The hot water system was a complicated series of solar collectors that they learned about in one of the pamphlets. With the income from the construction jobs and Maxie's waitress job in town, they were able to begin construction on the main building, a bunkhouse arrangement with showers and toilets. Next would come a dining hall and cookhouse. Eventually there would be a store to sell crafts and fresh vegetables. They sent word by the grapevine that they would welcome anyone interested in joining their effort who were willing to work, vegetarians only need apply.

People of all sorts and ages drifted in and out. Some stayed a few days and some stayed two or three years. Most contributed to the effort by working in the gardens or on whatever construction was currently in progress.

Maxi was the general administrator, but as time went by, others took up the jobs of food management or store and inventory management, etc. There were no posted rules and anyone could come and go, as they liked.

This being a drifter culture, there were always new faces in the dining hall. There was constant music, both recorded and live. It seemed like everybody played a guitar and some of them were very good.

The sense of community and freedom enriched those men, women and children who lived in the commune for whatever length of time in its hey-day.

Many of them followed the music and since music was Maxie's first love, she always knew who was playing where and usually managed to get to the concerts with two or three VWs or cars. All the kids went and slept in the cars or on blankets while their parents sang and passed joints around.

In 1969 the word was out that there was going to be a concert to end all concerts in upstate New York. It was to be held in Woodstock, a small artist community known for its Bohemian style.

Most of the current members of the commune determined to go. They gathered as much information as was available, arranged time off, packed up everybody in whatever vehicles were available and headed out across the country

They learned that the concert site had been moved from Woodstock to Bethel so they found that on their maps. They came up through Ohio and found the New York State Thruway and by the time they got to New York, it was obvious that every hippie, drifter, and druggie in America was on their way to this concert. There were thousands and thousands of vehicles choking the Thruway and every other road leading into Bethel.

The excitement grew and everybody began to feel that the world was one giant concert. There were whoops and grins and much passing of the pipe as they yelled back and forth from one vehicle to another, waiting for hours to get into the concert site. They were revved up and everybody was seeing people they hadn't seen in a while.

The party had begun! Eventually, they got to the site and were admitted. The massive platforms built for the performers were awesome and promised music beyond all expectations. The list of performers had grown to include most major pop musicians from everywhere. The music began, pot flowed freely, the rain came down and nobody cared. It was one hell of a wild and crazy party. For everybody there, who had run to some sort of personal freedom, this was it. A no holds-barred party with booze, pot, free love, no rules, and good, loud music.

They left Bethel hungry, filthy, and with massive hangovers but they had had a great time.

It was a few days before those who had been there were aware that the media was reporting the concert as a "LOVE·IN!"

There had been very little violence. Most everybody was stoned most of the time and they were there to have fun. The whole idea of the hippie movement was peace and love and it was no surprise to the people who had been there that there had been no violence. They were amazed that non-violence was even an issue. It was a party, man and it was groovy!

CHAPTER TWENTY FIVE

After "Woodstock," there were other concerts but they were forced efforts to repeat the "Woodstock" spirit. They were arranged by promoters anxious to cash in on this huge market of people who would pay big bucks to see their favorite performers. They jazzed up the concerts, sold merchandise, and after Altamont, made security so tight that the very thing Woodstock had stood for, freedom, was gone. When the music passed into the mainstream and became a "cash cow", the music got colder and more and more violent. It ushered in the "ME" generation with its attitude of "what's in it for me?"

There was no "day the music died," but it died and was replaced by a pale reflection played for profit. The vultures had taken over.

When the music died, drifting began to slow down. It was not so safe on the roads of America anymore. At the commune, they were hearing tales of hitchhiking boys and girls who had been murdered, raped or kidnapped. People stopped coming to the commune to crash for a few days. They were dropping back into the society they had dropped out of. (in answer to many a prayer of worried parents everywhere.)

The commune began to suffer money problems and there were so few people left that the work on the buildings didn't get done. By the time it closed in 1975, there were just Maxi, Jan, Heinz and Maxie's two children.

The principals in the original agreement had signed over their interest to Maxi when they left the commune. When she decided to sell the property, she made a considerable profit from the sale. After she had sent part of the profit to the original partners, she banked the rest. She bought a small house in town with a bedroom for each of the children and continued her job as a waitress.

CHAPTER TWENTY SIX

Maxi settled into a fairly conventional life. The kids went to public school; she worked forty hours a week and started going to church. She had been brought up in the Methodist church in Portland Valley and even though she had never felt the presence of any spiritual being, church seemed like a good place to take her children.

The congregation was small but friendly and active. There were families with children that went to school with her kids and people she saw every day in the diner where she worked. She was a bit suspect because of her hippie past, but the congregation gave her the benefit of the doubt.

By the time they had lived in town for a year, they were established in a pattern that was low key but satisfying. Their social life consisted of movies, TV, church and picnics together with a few friends.

Maxi had very little problem settling into this life. Her drifting days were over. She had a solid love and sense of responsibility for her children and she found herself doing things that would have formerly made her hair stand on end.

One Sunday morning as she was trying to get her family out the door to church and yelling at the kids to hurry up, she had a flashback to her childhood. She could remember her mother doing the exact same thing. She laughed and thought of all the other things that had changed in the past year.

She was not unhappy that things were as they were. She was forty-two and content with her life. She had spent twenty-four years in her travels and had met people she would never forget. Many she still kept in touch with.

She felt privileged to have lived as freely as she had and when she prayed in church, she was often thankful to whatever God she was supposedly praying to for all her experiences.

She was active in church in that she and the kids went to Sunday school and the church services on Sundays.

It was in Sunday school that she first got a glimmer of what might lie underneath this religion thing.

They were studying the "Historical Jesus" and trying to establish in their minds, the sort of political and physical environment in which Jesus had lived. Maxi entered into the discussion and felt a sense of knowledge of who this man might have been. He became less and less of an obscure and unreachable icon until, one day in class; she had a flash of recognition. She saw that Jesus had lived in a certain time and place but what he taught, "The Good News", or Gospel was eternal and contemporary. She began to understand what he had said and took to reading the Bible aided by reference books such as "The Interpreters Bible."

She was deeply engrossed in her reading one day, when she had a profound religious experience.

She was reading one of the reference books detailing "The Sermon On The Mount," when she felt a presence. She could either hear or feel, she could never define which, say to her "I am who I said I was." She thought "it must be Jesus," and she laughed to herself and thought of Bill Cosby"s routine when God announced himself to Noah and Noah asks, "Who are you really? Am I on Candid Camera?"

She felt the presence recede from her and she panicked and prayed that it would come back. She didn't know what she had done wrong, but evidently cynicism was not popular with Jesus.

Again, she felt that Jesus was there and He repeated, "I am who I said I was."

She made the commitment at that moment to follow this through to whatever end.

As the days and weeks went by, she read more and more and prayed constantly that she would be able to follow this spirit that she had come to believe in. She knew that her prior life had been preamble to a life lived in faith.

There was never any feeling of being a "better" person or running about doing "Good Works. "Indeed, she had the opposite experience. She felt that God loved her and knew her better than even she knew herself and that His promise was fulfillment and eternal life and any changes that occurred would be toward her true self.

She had read once, a small poem, about how the crowds roar when a rocket is launched, but nobody takes much notice when a flower blooms or a soul is born. She wasn't looking to be noticed; she had found her source.

CHAPTER TWENTY SEVEN

Mary Grace and Lila stayed in France for two years. After the first film was finished, she signed on with a French crew that was making a film to promote tourism in Europe. The economy was finally recovering from the war and airlines were bridging the Atlantic and dumping hordes of American tourists into Europe in ever-increasing numbers. A large tourist industry was set in motion and the American dollars brought in by tourists allowed funds for promotion.

The film would be sent to America and shown, along with brochures and lectures, to tour leaders and travel agents. Mary grace had been hired as Production Assistant. Her French had improved in the year she had been on the set of the first film and she now had practical knowledge of setting up a shoot and getting the best camera angles. She was learning every aspect of filmmaking and hoped, someday, to have her own production company. She made reams of notes on outlines for possible topics for future films and was leaning toward documentary films with social themes.

Its fair to say, her two years in France, caring for Lila and learning the business of making pictures, were the most intense years she had ever known. She fairly bristled with ideas and kept the crew on their toes.

When she was left in charge of the project because the manager was somewhere else, work went ahead at a good pace and her input helped make the film an award winning effort.

In the second year in France, Lila was enrolled in the local grammar school. Mary Grace hired a young girl to stay with them and when Mary Grace was away working on the picture, the girl stayed with Lila and made sure she was fed, clothed and got to school on time. As often as possible, Lila was on the set with her mother where she was well known and loved by the crew. They let her trail around with them and she learned much about filmmaking at a very early age. Lila had spoken French almost from the beginning of their stay in France and had absorbed the pronunciation and accent perfectly. By the time she was six she was bilingual. Mary Grace and Lila spent long weekends on bikes, picnicking and exploring.

Mary Grace had also bought a tiny Renault and they traveled whenever there was a break in shooting. They drove to Switzerland and Italy and across the border to Germany. There was so much to see and do and so many cuisine's to sample. Lila was an adventurous eater and loved the foods of Europe. When they were back in America, she was the only kid who brought Brie and grapes for lunch instead of peanut butter and jelly.

CHAPTER TWENTY EIGHT

When they got back to America, Mary Grace took a month off and went back to Portland Valley so that Lila could get to know her grandparents.

She called Nancy Lynn and they had lunch together. Nancy had three children and her husband; Adam worked for Nancy's father in the family Insurance Agency.

They seemed to have come disconnected in the years since they had seen each other. Nancy Lynn seemed somehow absent from herself and after they had reminisced over high school, there wasn't much left to talk about.

Mary Grace's mother had Nancy and her family over for a cookout and the four kids had a great time together.

Mary Grace remembered Adam from high school. He had been on the football team and was three years ahead of their class. She remembered that he had dated her sister for a while when he was a senior and she was a sophomore.

She reflected how much she loved Portland Valley and small towns in general. She described the small village in France where she had spent the last two years of her life to Adam and Nancy. Adam was very interested and asked many questions about everything. Nancy Lynn was amazed that anybody could just pick up and go halfway around the world with a four-year-old child.

Mary Grace remembered that Nancy had always been cautious. She realized that she was going deeper and deeper into caution and felt sorry for her. She wished that she could help her friend move forward and into life, but she didn't know how.

Shortly after that trip to Portland Valley, her parents moved to Chicago. Her father was a doctor and had decided to give up general practice and work in an inner city clinic. They had made investments that had paid off well and could afford to take a decrease in income while he "really practiced medicine" as he put it.

Mary Grace's two sisters were married. One lived in San Francisco. She was married to a successful commercial artist and had two boys. Her's was a rocky marriage and the one time Mary Grace and Lila visited them, the tension was so thick, that she decided not to go back for any length of time. When she was in San Francisco on business, she met her sister alone and they had lunch or went to the park to talk.

Her other sister was living in upstate New York. Her husband was an IBMer and had met Boot's husband at a conference in Germany. Her brother-in-law was not from Portland Valley so he didn't make the connection until he was talking to his wife and told her he had met Mike. She had figured out who he was and had her husband invite him for dinner the next time he was in town. She finally met him a year later. He had come to town on business and was invited to dinner. She had hoped to catch up on Portland Valley gossip, but Mike didn't seem to be too crazy about her hometown and didn't know any news.

CHAPTER TWENTY NINE

After her month's sabbatical, Mary Grace went back to New York and stayed with a friend at her apartment in the village while she found a place of her own. She enrolled Lila in a private school and since her funds were running low, she called her connections in the film industry and found out who was doing what.

Her reputation was good in the tight knit community of documentary filmmakers and she was known as a solid worker with a lot of talent. She was able to move immediately into a work in progress as director. The prior director had left in a huff in an argument over the budget-there wasn't enough money for him, and the project was in a shambles. There was much to do just to get the film back up off the ground.

The first thing Mary Grace did was to hire a new director and create a new position for herself as trouble-shooter. By the time the project was finished and the client was duly impressed, Mary Grace's reputation took an upswing and she had offers from several companies. She could pick and choose among very good projects at a high salary.

She was banking a large portion of her income at this point so that she would have a bankroll for her own company. She still needed backers and principals, but she would find what she needed, she was sure.

Her goal was to make documentary films that interested her. She wanted to show, on film, what it's like to be born poor and stay poor. She wanted to show the bridge between childhood and adulthood.

The world was in the throes of the social changes of the sixties and she wanted desperately to chronicle those changes.

She realized early on, that the counter-culture movement was a significant upheaval and would probably have lasting effects on the world culture and she wanted to report the effects of both sides of the revolution.

After Kennedy was shot in Dallas, she made up her mind to learn all she could about the theory of filmmaking. She wanted to make a lasting impact with her work and she didn't want to do sloppy work.

She met with the people who had already signed on with her in her budding company and told them of her plans. She appointed an assistant to be in charge of their first project and enrolled in the NYU doctoral program. She had weekly meetings with her crew and planned the locations. She burned the midnight oil to keep up with her classes and keep a tight rein on the film. The film was to be her doctoral thesis and she needed to have input into every aspect of the project so that it would qualify for the program.

The project was a documentary about the wine industry in New York State. There was barely enough money in the budget to travel to the Hudson Valley and to western New York to the Finger Lakes for filming, but they managed to presell the film to the chambers of commerce and tourist bureaus of the wine producing areas.

The film was a small success in the industry and she qualified for her Ph.D.

She was offered other ventures in the wine making industry to make trade films for use in the wineries as part of their tours. They were moderately successful and began to take on larger projects until finally, three years later; Mary Grace's dream to produce sociological films became reality.

Her company created and produced a film about graft in the Manhattan public schools system, which was aired in its entirety on NBC in prime time.

It caused a major shake-up in the school system and caused several watch dog committees to be formed within the city.

By the time the company had had the film on prime time TV, they were able to handle two projects at a time. There was much expansion of the company. People were glad to work for such a successful venture and Mary Grace was able to do more and more of the types of films she liked to do. She found herself in the enviable position of being able to have total creative freedom. As long as her company, ”Longacre,” was making money, she could indulge her desire to make dramatic pictures about the things that fascinated her. She made a trilogy of pictures about regional cuisine's in America and traveled all over the country to try the "best" local restaurant in any given area. She made contacts everywhere so that she could try the foods of a region in the homes of the people who lived there. Her food films were a hit wherever they were shown. They were intelligent and informed and humorous. Mary Grace was not one to take herself too seriously.

Lila was doing well in school but her favorite place to be was on the set with her mother. By the time she was eight, she already knew she would work in films too, and had sat in on more business meetings and creative brainstorming sessions than many an adult who had worked in the industry for years. She was able to provide ideas early on and was always welcomed by the others in the group. She didn't have many friends her own age and felt uncomfortable around most children. She had had whatever childhood she would ever have in France and seemed all the better for it. She never went through an awkward or rebellious stage and learned very early to work hard and do it right the first time.

CHAPTER THIRTY

While Mary Grace was at NYU, she had fallen in love with one of her professors.

He was a German director who had done some highly regarded films in Europe. Mary Grace had seen his films and had studied them as a graduate student and had met him before she had gone to France. The first time she had met him, he had been a consultant on the first film she had worked on in France. He advised the company on shooting in Europe and knew all the ropes to cut through the bureaucracy of the many European governments. He met with the crew in the New York office and Mary Grace kept an eye out for him when he was scheduled to be there for conferences.

She was very attracted to him but felt he was so far ahead of her that he would never notice her. He was also fifteen years older than she was and married. He was, nevertheless, a ladies man and more than one had fallen under his spell. Marriage didn't seem to inhibit his romantic activities at all.

Mary Grace was not aware of his wayward tendencies until much later, however. She just liked what she saw.

When she enrolled at NYU, he was her advisor for her thesis and she worked closely with him over the period of her graduate work.

He was newly divorced by this time and Mary Grace made up her mind that she would have him. She sought him out for coffee and kept an eye on his whereabouts at the university. He was surprisingly easy to capture and before too long, they were dating.

Everything took on a new reality during this period. She allowed herself to fall completely in love with Reuters. Her relationship with Lila's father had been washed out over the years and she felt like a new person, in love for the very first time.

She would never again hear the top pop songs from that year and not be transported back to that winter when she was so captured by her romance with Reuters.

She was never sure if they had actually been in love or if they were just in the midst of a hormonal explosion of massive proportions. They fell on each other like animals that had been starved for weeks. Mary Grace was very limited in sexual experience and was amazed at herself. She experienced for the first time; raw, uninhibited sex and she loved it! The novelty of living out her fantasies was enough to keep the affair alive and she did not bother to look at other aspects of Reuter's personality. In the spring of that year, he told Lila that she and Reuters were going to get married. Lila liked him and was glad to see her mother so happy. They were married in June and he moved into her apartment since it was larger than his was.

They had been married a year when Mary Grace got pregnant. She was torn between the need for freedom for her career and the real joy at the prospect of another baby. Reuters, on the other hand, was not pleased. He had three teenage children already by his first wife and did not want any more.

Things began to fall apart during her pregnancy. Reuters had begun to resent being tied down and had started an affair with one of his students. When Mary Grace learned of his perfidy, she was devastated. She still believed that you shouldn't cheat on your mate. To say that this was a painful time for her was to say that cutting off an arm stings a bit. Before their son, Eric, was born, Reuters had moved out and was living with the student. They were divorced exactly two years after they were married.

Mary Grace was determined to get to know Eric before he was four years old as she had done with Lila. Lila adored her brother and was old enough to help take care of him. The three of them spent much time on the sets of films in progress. Mary Grace hired young men and women to take care of Eric on the set and she was always available in a crisis.

From the very beginning, Eric exhibited a winning personality and responded joyfully to all the attention he got from his mother and sister and the people on the various sets. He looked like Reuters with his blond hair and blue eyes. Most everybody was drawn to him and he loved being the center of attention, which was most of the time.

It was a long time before Mary Grace understood what had happened with her relationship with Reuters. Her hurt was a long time healing and the process could only begin when she could see the whole picture from a distance of several years.

She learned that morality is not a standard issue item and that true morality is practiced in love and maturity.

After a while, she no longer hated Reuters. She understood that there was something in his make-up, good, bad or indifferent, that didn't allow him to be faithful. She didn't know if he could overcome the problem, but she forgave him so that she could get on with her life. She knew that he hurt himself as much as he hurt others.

CHAPTER THIRTY ONE

Nancy Lynn had taken her role as hostess seriously and drafted Jean to help her get the house ready for her guests.

Jean was married to one of the agents in her father's insurance office and had not worked outside the home since her two children, John and David were born. She was determined that she would not be an emotionally void parent like her mother had been and she made sure that her sons spent time with both of her parents.

Actually, Nancy Lynn was a good grandmother. Since she was not responsible for them, she was relaxed and loving with them. She had great patience and taught them to work in the yard with her. They helped her weed the flowerbeds and plant tulips and daffodils in the fall. She had enrolled them in the stable where she had taken riding lessons and often went to watch them ride.

They spent weekends with her so that Jean and her husband could get away. She had put them to work in the back yard cleaning out an area where she wanted to plant perennials and shrubs and they had worked like little beavers for her.

To get ready for her house party, Nancy Lynn decided she needed new towels and linens. Jean made new curtains for the kitchen and bathrooms. There was much decision-making that went into choosing the right colors and fabrics. She and Jean and Jean's friend Susan went to Salton City to a huge mall and spent an entire day shopping and lunching. Margaret had called with a list of things that still needed to be done for the reunion and Nancy Lynn met with the reunion committee and took on the job of planning the entertainment for the dinner. She had a committee of three and they met at her house to begin planning the program.

She had been alone so long and had steeped herself in so much bitterness and self-pity that she, and every one else, had forgotten that she had a keen sense of humor. When she began to work with her former classmates and they began to remember some of the people in the class and their teachers, they spent so much time laughing at their reminiscences that they had to force themselves back to work. They finally came up with a skit to be performed by members of the class who had indicated they were coming. They wrote letters to the classmates with their portion of the script and were warned not to discuss their lines with any other attendee. There were wild references to things that had happened in high school as well as to what had happened to them since.

There was not a lot of information as to their present lives for some of the graduates, but some scenarios were simply made up as suppositions as to what might have happened based on their high school days.

So much had happened to the world in forty years and those people who had survived the changes had lived lives of discovery and challenge. There was much to be said about them, and some of it was very funny.

Nancy had elicited enough information from her friends to skewer them royally. Mary Grace, in particular, was to get an especially comic send-up because of her success. The committee had pieced together bits and pieces of some of her films to make a comic and non-sensical montage that was hilarious.

By the time the committee had finished the program, each classmate would be included and would have a part in the skits, and nobody but the committee had any idea what was going on.

Each morning when Nancy Lynn took her coffee out to the screened porch, she now took her portable phone and list upon list. She worked as she ate and then began phoning to get her day organized. She had taken on the job of notifying the classmates of their part in the program and had received return mail asking questions and sending greetings. She read the letters to the reunion committee and made sure that someone answered each one if not herself.

She was so immersed in getting her house ready for her friends and with plans for the reunion that she was not aware of the changes that had taken place in her day to day life. She was involved in activities that came naturally to her because she was involved with people who had been her friends in the best part of her life, her years at Portland Valley Central High School.

She was at home among these people and their friendship and acceptance of her made her look anew at what she had been so fearful of. After talking with her friends, she could see that life is not to hide from but to enter into.

She didn't really understand why she had been the way she was and she didn't really understand that she was making her way out of her little world where she was safe but dead, but she was stepping out and doing so with humor and grace.

Jean was the only one who truly saw the changes in Nancy. Her sons knew that their Grandmother was more accessible to them, but they took the changes for granted. Jean, however, was profoundly grateful for her "new" mother!

CHAPTER THIRTY TWO

Jean had told Adam all the things her mother was involved in and Adam was, quite naturally, astonished.

After the divorce, he had moved to the other side of town. He had insisted that Nancy Lynn return to her maiden name, as he was totally fed up with being her keeper. He had done everything he could to keep his family together and had never been unfaithful or cruel to her. When the children had all grown up, he sat her down and told her that he was moving out to live his own life. He was tired of taking care of a forty eight-year-old child and that if she never grew up, he no longer cared.

He had been basic and to the point but he barely touched Nancy with the truth of what he was saying. She took his rejection as one more horror that she couldn't deal with.

Adam bought a house in a new development and began to make a life for himself. He dated several women in town and was considered a good catch. He had plenty of money and had matured into a handsome and distinguished looking man. His children and grandchildren adored him. He took them to special occasions and remembered to bring gifts when he traveled. He took trips alone or with his current woman friend and he relished the freedom from the responsibility to care for Nancy.

The agency had prospered under his management and he had sent money to Nancy's parents as per their agreement when the agency had been turned over to him. He had visited them in Florida several times since the divorce and they still considered him their son-in-law.

When Nancy's parents thought about her, they took responsibility for her immaturity, because that was how they saw it. They had loved her and still loved her, but she drained the very life out of them. They did not look forward to her visits to Florida and were relieved when she left. They felt pity and irritation for her because of her self-involvement, but they were powerless to help her as she whined and raved about Adam and then went back to Portland Valley.

They were in their eighties now and had made their peace about Nancy Lynn. They saw their great-grandchildren once or twice a year and felt that Nancy had done something right anyway. They were very proud of her family.

CHAPTER THIRTY THREE

It is true that, eventually, you have to take responsibility for your own life, Nancy mused. She was standing at the bedroom window and noticing how pretty the stand of trees looked in their late spring finery. She had seen the individual components of the grove, the trees and flowers, the cardinal and the other animals and now she saw the grove as an entity. Everything fit together and each part was important to the whole. Without each separate thing, everything else was diminished from lack of that contribution.

She was beginning to see that all of life was like that. We are nourished by each other and the world of people around us.

She thought about the house she lived in, the roads she drove on, even the car she drove and realized for the first time, that all of her world was made by people who shared their talents and time to develop the things that she had always taken for granted. She felt that she had contributed so little to society and wondered how she could never have seen the world as she was beginning to see it now.

She lived in a house built by others, drove on safe roads designed by people she didn't even know and shopped in buildings created by people who wanted to express themselves or earn a living. How had she been able to survive when she had been so totally out of the loop? She was sad that she was fifty-eight years old before she had figured this out. She wondered where the truth had been hiding all this time.

It probably hadn't been hiding at all. She had just gotten to where it was evident and now she could see it.

CHAPTER THIRTY FOUR

Boots was looking for a leather two-suiter that she had bought years ago. All the luggage was kept in the attic, but the piece she wanted was not with the other luggage. She went back downstairs to look again in the closets and the basement. She was about to give up and bring down another suitcase from the attic when she spotted the leather case in a corner of the furnace room. She picked it up and dusted it off and went back to the bedroom to store it there so that she would have it when she was ready to pack for the reunion. There was something in the bag and she opened it to clean it out.

There were several business letters all addressed to Mike. She opened one of them and saw that it was dated ten years ago. They were from a former manager of Mike's and the one she read first was a job review. The manager was very negative about Mike's performance and had given him a terrible rating.

She read each of the letters. There were four in all, and she saw where Mike's job had been in serious jeopardy for a period of six months. The final letter had put him on notice that he would have to shape up or ship out.

She tried to remember ten years ago and if Mike had given her any indication that he was in deep trouble at work and she couldn't remember one incident that would have given her a clue.

Her first reaction was one of sadness that she had not been able to be there for Mike when he was having a problem that surely hurt him where he was most vulnerable.

She wondered what he had done to save his job and if he had had to kow-tow to management. She knew that he was capable and likely to grovel when he was threatened. She had once threatened to leave him and he had been so pathetic that she had never mentioned the possibility again.

"God!" she thought," Will there ever be any honesty in this marriage?" What was it about him or her that caused them to live together and raise a family and never have a clue who the other was. She didn't know if she should ask him about the letters or just pretend that she had never seen them.

She had had enough pretending by now, though, so she put them on her desk. She would talk to him about them later.

CHAPTER THIRTY FIVE

Boots had lately started to wish that her nickname had not stuck with her so long. Very few people knew that her name was actually Barbara Kate. She had been named for two favorite aunts, sisters of her mother. The family had called her Boots ever since she was two and one of the aunts had given her a pair of cowboy boots. She loved them and wore them until they were too small for her.

By the time she had outgrown the boots, she was being called "Boots" and the nickname stuck long after the cowboy boots were history.

She had never considered that her childhood nickname might be inappropriate and had never tried to get anyone to call her Barbara. She was beginning to realize that her nickname was one other way that she had failed to grab on to something that was really her. She wondered if she could get anybody to call her Barbara at this stage of her life but decided it would be too much hassle.

When Mike came home from work that night, he had news about the downsizing at IBM. The company was offering very good packages as incentives to employees to take early retirement. Someone Mike's age could retire with nearly the same income as a person of sixty-five.

There was a sense of urgency among the IBM establishment. Long term employees were trying to figure out how long the offer would last before the company would get serious and start laying people off.

Mike came home with the notion of talking to Boots about his idea to retire this year. He had worked out the figures for his settlement and had a printout of income based on their savings, stock and the money he would receive as an incentive. It was very do-able and he was anxious to show Boots the figures he had come up with.

She was on the phone when he came in and when she was finished; she went into the bedroom where he was changing. She had the letters with her. She told him that she had found them in the suitcase and asked him to tell her about the incident at work when he had nearly lost his job. Mike had the retirement issue on his mind and the letters were ancient history. He had gotten past that problem and rarely thought about it. He wanted to forget the whole thing and talk about the retirement plans with Boots.

This looked suspiciously like every other issue they should have discussed over the years and she was not going to let it go by. How could they possibly talk about their future when they didn't even know how to talk about their past? She was determined that they would have a dialogue about the letters and told him that she was going to fix their dinner and that he was to re-read the letters. They would talk about them after dinner. Her issue of this ultimatum left no room for disagreement.

He decided to do as she suggested. After dinner, she cleared the table, poured coffee and asked him to read the first letter. By the time he had read each of the letters aloud, he was obviously upset. His hands were shaking and he had to stop reading before he had finished reading the last letter. The letters brought back a feeling of humiliation.

He never wanted to tell Boots how he had had to grovel to keep his job. The job had been in jeopardy mainly because he'd had a manager who simply didn't like him and had made his life miserable for two years

It had never occurred to Mike to talk to Boots about his problems at work. He needed to be King of his castle and Kings did not grovel. His home was truly his castle and he didn't bring anything home with him that might upset that life where he was safe and free from stress.

Boots had always made their home a sanctuary for him and the kids and he had always assumed that was the way things were supposed to be. He was a bit slower than Boots and it took him longer to realize what they had done to each other.

As he told her the whole sad story of the incident at work, he began to cry. He had not cried since he was ten years old and he felt out of control but relieved. Boots urged him to continue and tell her the whole story. He understood that she wanted to hear only the truth from him and he continued until he had told her everything.

She sat across from him at the table and looked at him for a few minutes. He was beginning to wonder if she was disgusted with him and started to get up and go upstairs. She stopped him and he sat back down.

She began to tell him all that had been going through her mind. He was amazed to hear her speak at such great length and so coherently. He couldn't even follow all that she was saying and he wondered where this woman had been hiding all these years. He reached across the table and took her hands in his. He seemed to need to absorb what she was saying because he could understand enough to realize that this was one of the crossroads of life where it behooves one to keep alert and make decisions very carefully.

She talked for two hours and he listened, mostly. Her thoughts came easily and she spoke with the ring of truth and with an underlying urgency.

After two hours, she stopped. Mike still held her hands and he struggled to say something, but there was too much to take in and he couldn't say anything. Finally, he told her that he was too overwhelmed to enter into any kind of dialogue tonight. He would not go to the office tomorrow and try to sort out his thoughts so that he could have some sort of rational input into this new awareness of hers.

Boots went to bed and slept the most peaceful sleep she had slept in years and Mike sat in the chair in the family room and let his castle come tumbling down around his head.

The next morning, after breakfast, they dressed for walking. They stayed out all morning long, walking, stopping for coffee and talking.

It was a beautiful spring day and new life was all around them. As they walked and talked, they often held hands and were oblivious to the world around them.

CHAPTER THIRTY SIX

Sally first met Jim when he was married to Alice. Alice was a client who was very social and had four major parties each year and Sally had catered most of them. There was always a theme and much money was spent for food, flowers and decorations. She and Sally always had a planning session as soon as one party was finished to begin planning for the next one.

There had been seasonal parties, costume parties and parties just for the heck of it.

Jim was in on some of the planning, but the parties were primarily Alice's bailiwick-a way to keep her busy.

While they were planning a retirement party for old friends, Alice mentioned that she had met another couple recently that she was inviting to the party they were planning. She didn't say if they were friends of the guests of honor or not, but she talked about them frequently. When she told Sally they were coming to the party, there was a definite note of excitement in her voice. Alice seemed to find reasons to mention the new couple often. His name was Paul and hers, Betty. By the time the party was in the last phases of planning, Sally knew that Alice was either involved with Paul or deeply interested in him.

Sally met Paul and Betty the night of the party. She was in the kitchen directing her staff in the distribution of hors d'ouvres when she had to go out to the truck to get more punch. She nearly fell over Alice and Paul standing by the truck. They were locked in a passionate embrace and hadn't seen Sally approach.

The cat was obviously out of the bag at this point. It seemed that Alice and Paul had planned to tell their respective mates that they were in love and wanted a divorce so they could marry each other.

Within weeks, their divorce and marriage were a "fait accompli" and they had moved to Ohio.

After the marriage of Alice, Jim often stopped by Sally's to cry on her shoulder. Eventually, he got involved with helping her prepare for parties. She often joked that she would have to put him on the pay roll. They worked well together and had fun trying to find new ways to serve the same foods over and over. Sometimes he helped her serve at parties and clean up. They would rehash the party afterwards with her staff and make suggestions and comments. Jim was a welcome addition to the group and had valuable comments to add to the discussion. After a time they started to go out socially as a couple. They loved movies and walking and they spent hours talking.

Jim had three children who were all in college or married and Cal was on his own and married to Joan.

They had formed a strong bond of friendship and when they drifted into a romantic relationship, it was quite natural. They were comfortable together and laughed often. Jim was the first to mention the possibility of marriage. Sally didn't say no and they considered life without each other and realized that the love and friendship they shared made a solid basis for marriage.

They were married in the spring with all their children in attendance. Sally's partner catered the reception and they went to Greece for their honeymoon.

Neither had ever expected to have a happy, married relationship again. Jim had taken a long time to heal after his marriage had broken up and Sally was still unable to consider losing someone else she loved, so they were surprised at the happiness they found in each other.

Theirs' was a union based first of all on friendship. They were always glad to be with each other and had much in common. They loved sharing each day's discoveries with the other and talked late into the night sometimes over a sink filled with vegetables to be prepped or pans and pans of miniature canapés to put together.

There was passion too. Their sexual relationship had begun early on in the friendship and they were nourished by the intimacy and surprised that sex should be so gratifying at their age. He was fifty and she was forty-eight.

Sally had loved sex with Clarence, but had considered the act as primarily procreative. With her childbearing years behind her, sex became more an act of love and intimacy.

Their relationship was founded on friendship however, and they stayed good friends after their marriage.

The black pit left by the death of Clarence and their children gradually filled in with time. There would never be a day that Sally didn't miss them but sometimes she was grateful that they had been together as long as they had.

Jim could not have known how terrible those years after the accident had been for her and he didn't pretend that he did. He simply listened when she finally talked to him about it. He wept with her when she talked about the awful realization that they were never coming back.

They crossed a barrier in their life together and the experience brought them closer.

CHAPTER THIRTY SEVEN

The nearer to the reunion date, the more excited Maxi got. She had called Sally to make sure she was coming and had gotten out all her albums and had chosen pictures of her life over the years. She had found a box of photographs of their high school years and had laughed at their clothes and hair styles, but they were so young and beautiful in their innocence. She couldn't wait to see everyone and show them the pictures.

How she had managed to save the pictures in all her years of drifting, she couldn't say, but she had always managed to hang on to what was important, both literally and figuratively. She had desired freedom not escape.

Six years after she had settled in town, she had used the rest of the money from the sale of the commune to buy a commercial building and open a book store/coffee house. She had been on the leading edge with her store and had prospered. People were enchanted with the idea of reading and having coffee after shopping, and business people would often forgo lunch at the diner in favor of salads and sandwiches at Maxie's. Her daughter did all the food preparation and kept the menu updated with trendy offerings and fresh, inventive salads. Tex/mex food was very popular and nachos and tacos were easy to prepare and delicious. She cornered the market for California avocados in the area.

Maxi selected the books and set up a corner for tapes and periodicals. After CDs became popular, she kept a large selection of folk and Children's stories. There were story hours for children and book readings for adults. Through her connection with Jake, she was able to have several authors come and read parts of their books.

Eventually she expanded to include a section of computer software. Her son was a computer buff and kept her up to date on the latest innovations and trends. Her store was a great place to spend an hour or two, eating, browsing and buying.

She had written several articles and essays that had been published in magazines dealing with alternative lifestyles. There was a large market in the Southwest for people still looking for a way out of the mainstream and Maxi spoke to the possibilities. Jake had been helpful in her writing endeavors. He had proofread her works and offered suggestions and comments on style and grammar. He had stopped writing for several years and had lived in Switzerland for that period. He had never married and neither had Maxi, but they had shared the children and Jake contributed much financially. He often took one or the other on trips which they had loved when they were young.

He had begun writing again in his forties and had been very successful. He was always a favorite when he came to Maxie's to read and sign autographs.

Maxi had become a valuable part of the business community. She often thought that she had made a 360-degree turn somewhere in her life without ever realizing she was turning. She was still living as honestly as she could and had not compromised herself to get anything she might want. She was happy with who she was.

Maxi had named her daughter Sunflower and her son Falcon. They hated their names when they started to public school and had taken a lot of heat from other kids with names like John and Susan and Buck. It had been painful for Maxi to see them hurt by the words of others and she had been at a loss for a solution. She sat them down and explained what their names had meant to her and Jake when they were born. Their names were given to celebrate their lives and the joy of their parents.

"Sunflower" was both a hope for the future and a description of her beauty. "Falcon" was so named for his newborn personality. He rarely cried and seemed always to be watching and listening. He had grown into his name and was at home outdoors with other natural creatures.

They understood early that life is much more than what is evident on the surface and eventually became proud of their names and what they represented.

There were times in junior high school when they wished they had more conventional names like other kids, but they discovered that "other" kids were individuals too, and that their name was a surface detail, not the real person. They tended to appreciate the differences in people, not their sameness. Since they were always encouraged to be themselves, they were more comfortable with people who were unencumbered by a fake persona to hide their true selves.

Maxi loved them with a deep, almost painful, love and turned to them for companionship and friendship. They responded in kind and when they married, they stayed in the town where they had lived since the commune had folded. Their children, however, had been given traditional names and they often envied their parent's more colorful and beautiful names.

CHAPTER THIRTY EIGHT

Mary Grace got back to the hotel at five after a satisfying day spent in SoHo with Eric and Hannah, his wife. They had lived in New York for five years where Eric worked as an actor. He had had some success on Broadway and TV. He was a very handsome, with his father's blond hair and blue eye. He had a solid relationship with his mother and his father and the eight half siblings of his father's various liaisons. He and Lila were best friends.

Reuters had married twice more after he and Mary Grace had divorced. He had a child by each of those wives and three others born of liaisons that did not culminate in marriage.

He had managed to keep a healthy career going throughout and had done some fine work in film. After he had retired from teaching, he had acted, as consultant, on many films including some that Mary Grace had been involved with. He lived alone now in an apartment on the upper West Side and was slightly senile and a little eccentric. Even Mary Grace had learned to love him again.

Eric had not inherited Reuter's talent but he was over-endowed with charm and good looks and some acting ability. He made a decent living as an actor, but had come to the conclusion that he would never be a big star. He was happy being second lead in TV dramas and character parts in movies.

Eric had married a writer seven years ago and had two daughters. He was the very model of devotion and fidelity. He loved his family and was involved with his daughters' daily care. His wife was the tough one in the family and made sure they all toed the line on behavior, chores and fulfillment of responsibility.

Mary Grace loved Hannah and laughed when she saw her ordering Eric through his paces. She and Lila had spoiled him rotten and he had always been able to charm either one of them into whatever he wanted. Hannah was exactly right for him and, to his credit, he knew it. They lived in SoHo and had friends from all areas of the arts and the media.

Lila had lived in France for fifteen years. She lived with Jean Claude who had been a production manager on a film she directed. They had two children, a boy named Jean Martin and a girl named Adela. Theirs was a stormy, volatile relationship.

Lila was a director by profession and had worked in every country in the world. She had spent months in China on one project and had directed in Africa, Cuba and the Caribbean. She had done specialty pieces on all the Olympics since 1984.

She loved work and Jean Claude was often left alone to fend for himself and the children when they weren't with Lila. He was very European and chauvinistic and hated not having the upper hand in the relationship. His whole effort, however, was lost on Lila. She had been very independent most of her life and had been encouraged to do what she did best. She was very good at what she did and had every intention of doing as much as she could.

Jean Claude had fallen in love with her independence and he stayed in love with her independence and realized he couldn't have it both ways, but he still complained bitterly when she was off on some far-flung location. Lila was used to his inconsistencies and told him often that he could leave whenever he'd had enough. This attitude truly infuriated him. He could have any woman he wanted and she and he knew it but Lila was the one he wanted. The kids were used to the fighting and even though they hated the loudness, they had decided to let the matter rest with their parents. They were never seriously afraid their parents would separate anyway because it was obvious to anyone that they loved each other.

Her daughter's independence and willfulness amused Mary Grace. She was not involved in any small town value system. She always knew what she wanted and, usually, how to get it.

Mary Grace and Lila had worked together on several projects and Mary Grace had learned to defer to her daughter on many occasions.

Lila had gotten her undergraduate degree in film while working continuously on one project or another. She had decided not to go for a graduate degree because she was in demand at an early age for projects all over the world. She had picked up enough in the countries she had worked in to be conversant in French, Spanish, German and Russian and could get around in any country she happened to find herself in. She was one of the youngest professionals in the business and the only woman to have such clout-and use it! Mary Grace was proud of her daughter's accomplishments and she and Lila were close. Mary Grace saw her often on business and she loved to visit the family in France.

They had both been at home in France since the two years they had spent there when Lila was four.

Lila would be at the awards dinner tonight and would be arriving at Kennedy any minute. She was to stay with Mary Grace in her hotel and they would have two days to spend together. They were to have dinner tomorrow at Eric and Hannah's and visit mutual friends who had a house in Bridgehampton.

The children were still in school, so Jean Claude was staying behind in France. The French school system frowned on interruption of school unless there was a very good reason. Jean Claude had acquiesced easily enough to this plan. He could actually see the rationale behind their frequent separations, but old attitudes have a way of taking hold, settling in and hanging on.

He had lately begun to realize that he liked to have the children when Lila was away. They had their own way of doing things and enjoyed one another's company.

Adela had decided to plan a welcome home dinner for her mother and Jean Martin was to help her. Jean Claude was an excellent cook and would supervise the preparations. In his most rational moments, he knew he was as happy as he had ever been.

CHAPTER THIRTY NINE

Mary Grace and Lila had arrived at the hotel where the awards dinner was being held a few minutes early to see old friends. There were people from all over the world representing the cream of the crop in international documentary film production. Mary Grace was impressed by the turnout of high-level producers, backers, directors, etc. She hadn't realized that this was such an important function.

There were representatives from PBS and various big foundations that funded documentary films and there were people from the news media and the entertainment cartel.

Mary Grace began to wonder if she had dressed appropriately for the occasion. It was almost overwhelming.

After the dinner, the awards ceremony started and Mary Grace accepted the award for best domestic film, a picture she had produced with an American crew in Chicago about the effects of urban blight on that city's inner city inhabitants.

After the awards had been presented, the chairman came to the podium to announce a special award for lifetime achievement in documentary/short form films.

Mary Grace wondered who the honoree could be. As she listened to the speaker list the credits, she realized they were talking about her. There happened to be a camera trained on her when it dawned on her and the resulting video of the path of emotions that crossed her face as the truth sunk in was bound to be a family classic.

The committee had known she would never have accepted the award if she had known beforehand, so they had conspired with Lila to make sure she was at the dinner and that she knew nothing about the award.

When they finally named her as the recipient of the award, she had no choice but to accept, which she did most graciously. Indeed, she was touched at the love and honor bestowed upon her by the award and she was especially gratified that Lila had been so involved with all the arrangements.

She had no prepared acceptance speech, naturally, so she had to wing it. Her words of sincere thanks came easily as well as her thanks to all the hundreds of people she had worked with over the years.

It was when she began to tell about how wonderful it had been to do something she loved as much as she did her job that she stalled and a lump came to her throat. She had been fortunate to do what she loved to do. Her career had given her the opportunity to express how she felt about the changing cultures she had lived through and chronicle those changes. She was humbled by the award and said as much to the attendees. She was totally sincere and those in the audience appreciated the sincerity. At the end of her speech, they rose as one and gave her a standing ovation from their collective hearts.

She was a basket case and Lila had to steer her off to the bathroom so that she could get herself back together again.

She hugged Lila and thanked her. She was wiped out.

CHAPTER FORTY

Nancy Lynn was driving home from Margaret's house. She had gone to pick up letters from classmates about their part in the reunion entertainment. The script had grown to include all the classmates and some of the spouses, especially those who had dated their mates in high school.

As she drove onto the highway, she passed the riding stable and had a thought. She turned the car around at the next driveway and headed back to the stable. As she parked in the lot, she felt the same excitement she always felt when she came to the stables. She had loved riding and had taken lessons until she was fourteen. Her parents had bought her a horse, which had been kept at the stable, and she had tended to the animal daily. In addition to her lessons, she rode every morning before school and two or three times a week she had come after school to groom the horse or to go on trail rides with other kids who had horses there. There was literally nothing she did not like about riding horses. She never minded mucking out the stalls or grooming the horse when she had gotten muddy. She was as good a rider as she had been a swimmer.

When she brought her grandsons for their lessons, she always felt at home, but she had never considered riding again. As she had passed by the stable, she had the overwhelming urge to go back and check out the schedule for adult classes.

As she drove into the parking lot, she began to feel foolish and very old, but she parked the car and got out and went towards the business office. She could see several horses out in the fields and as she neared the indoor arena, she could hear the instructor urging someone to "ask for the canter" and again "NOW! ASK FOR THE CANTER!" A thrill like an electrical charge went through her as she remembered riding over fences at a canter and the easy, effortless landing on the other side. She had taken to jumping as easily as walking and had been encouraged to enter all the shows where she had done well, taking a whole trophy case of ribbons and trophies.

She walked into the business office and told Pam, the general manager, that she wanted to know if there were lessons for older people like her. As it turned out, there were several classes for adults ranging from the low twenties to seventy-five. They were scheduled at least once a week and could be taken three times weekly.

She made arrangements to come in the next day, wearing appropriate attire, to test her level of ability so the instructor would know where to place her. She had not ridden in forty-five years, so it was safe to assume that she would be considered a novice again. When she got up the next morning, she felt excited and eager. She was to be at the stable by ten so she dug out jeans, a tee shirt and a pair of loafers left over from years ago. They were the only shoes she had that had heels to keep her feet from slipping out of the stirrups.

She was too excited to eat breakfast and decided to go early to the stable to find out which horse she was to ride and to get to know him somewhat.

The horse they had chosen for her was a big, gentle mare named "Maris" and Nancy Lynn approved. She checked the saddle and stirrups and walked around the horse to see if everything was as it should be. She tightened the girth and patted the horse on the nose and spoke gently to her.

As she talked to the horse, she thought about the animals in her yard that she spoke to and saw a connecting link between the "civilized" world and the animal kingdom. She could not be a part of the wild kingdom of animals but here was a crossover from one world to the other. She wondered if her interest in the wild animals had not begun with her love of horses. At any rate, she felt very much at home here.

When the instructor came and took her to the arena, she walked "Maris" over and when she got to the center she used the mounting block and was astride. She settled in, found her seat and felt as if she had been riding all her life. She started the horse in a walk and went several times around the perimeter. The instructor asked her if she wanted to trot and Nancy Lynn squeezed and chirked and Maris trotted around the rink at a gentle pace. Nancy started to post automatically and found the rhythm immediately. She was riding with increasing confidence and feeling comfortable.

She reined up by the instructor when asked and dismounted.

After she had walked the horse back to the stable and helped the groom unsaddle her and rub her down, she sat down with Pam and the instructor and talked about a lesson schedule. It was decided that she would start in a novice class until she was "broken in" again and then would progress up until she found her level. She was to start in two days and would come twice a week to start.

It had all been so business like that Nancy didn't realize she had been suppressing her excitement until she got into her car and began to go over her brief ride. The memory of trotting around the track brought a feeling of victory somehow and she grinned to herself thinking, "maybe you can teach an old dog, almost new tricks!"

CHAPTER FORTY ONE

Sally sat at the kitchen table making lists for her partner and Jim. She would be away from home for a week and Jim had decided to stay away from the office in the mornings to lend a hand with the catering business. He was a lawyer and his practice could afford for him to be away now that he was thinking of retirement. He was glad to let the young Turks take over. He had worked twelve-hour days for weeks on end in his younger days and did not miss that hectic schedule.

He liked the totally different work atmosphere of Sally's catering kitchen. There were moments of absolute hysteria just before a party, but Sally had everything organized so well that most every thing got done on schedule, and the clean up and post-mortems were relaxed. Everybody usually sat around Sally's table with a glass of wine and leftover party goodies and made lists of suggestions. She had been following this ritual since she first started the business and they still always had suggestions and corrections. This was also a chance for everybody to unwind and air grievances. Her's was a congenial group and she managed to keep a crew far longer than most catering and restaurant businesses.

As far as Sally knew, all the girls in the group were flying to Portland Valley and would meet at Nancy Lynn's the Wednesday before the Saturday night reunion dinner.

Margaret and Glen were having a cocktail party at their house Friday night and the entire group had been invited. Nancy Lynn had alluded to the entertainment and a rehearsal for some of the graduates who would be coming in time for a Saturday afternoon get- together.

Mary Grace had suggested that they all do dinner together at Nancy Lynn's house Thursday night and she would help cook it. She was also bringing a camera crew to film the reunion as a gift to each of the graduates.

According to Nancy, they would make out a menu and shop for the ingredients for the Thursday night dinner in the morning and spend the afternoon touring all their old hangouts (those that still existed) and spend the evening cooking, eating and talking. There would be no early wakeup time for Friday, so they could talk all night to catch up on forty years of their individual lives.

None of the group was coming with a husband or significant other, so their time would be for each other.

Sally was more and more looking forward to the week and seeing her friends. She had never considered how important her high school years had been in her development, but she remembered so much more about those years than other phases of her life. Those years were as free of adult pressures as she had ever been. She was happy and busy and popular and her memories of that time were very good. She wanted to "go back home" and be a kid again for a weekend. She was glad that Jim wouldn't be there. He had mentioned that he would go if she wanted him to, but she could see that he was happier at home helping with the catering business and putting in a few hours a day at the office.

He always had work to do there and would spend the afternoons helping other attorneys prepare cases for trial. He took fewer and fewer cases on his own now but he was a great resource because of his past experience. He was not above doing research either, if another lawyer needed it.

Jim was actually looking forward to being on his own and being lord of the whole domain. He was used to deferring to Sally for the house and her business and he was eager to check out some ideas of his own.

Sally thought it funny that he was so excited for her to go. She was aware that he had lots of ideas for her business, but had never said too much. She could sense his excitement when he wanted to change a procedure but even in the suggestion sessions, he often held back. Sally was looking forward to seeing what he would do while she was away.

She also realized that time apart would be good for the marriage. Since they had been married, there had never been a day when they were separated. They both seemed to feel that their union was a Godsend and for most of their marriage, they had needed each other so much just to get past their respective hurts from the past. They were at a point now though, where they felt comfortable with each other and themselves. A lot of healing and growth had taken place over the ten years of the marriage.

Sometimes Sally felt that her life had been a long continuous journey just trying to figure out why she hurt so much and to solve all the problems that had caused the hurt.

Her natural bent was toward happiness. She had never been negative and except for the period after Clarence died, she was not bitter.

Her happiness with Jim was in some ways suspect. She kept waiting for the other shoe to drop and some horrible event to crush her joy.

Lately, though, she was realizing that she could not control outside events. She was responsible for her own actions and that was the limit of her control, so she concluded that she would get the most out of every day and love Jim and her life to the fullest. If something happened to shatter that happiness, she would have no regrets. That was pretty much the way she had lived most of her life anyway, so she would just continue doing the same thing

CHAPTER FORTY TWO

"I guess I must have grown up," mused Boots as she packed the last pair of panty hose in her luggage. She had finished her shopping and laundry for the reunion, cleaned the house and made sure the kid down the street would come to mow the lawn while she was away. She had always taken care of the house and had been very good at the job. She had good work habits and knew before it was too late, when something needed replacing or repairing.

She had a long list of reliable people to call on when something broke. It had never occurred to her to let Mike do anything with the maintenance of the house. He was no mechanic and the few times he had tried to repair something ("to save money", he said) the item usually had to be replaced. When she looked around now to check everything out, she had a sense of satisfaction. Even though her lot in life had been chosen for her, she had learned it and done a good job.

She had made plans; now, to find something that was her choice. She wanted to explore the possibilities of other places and things. She didn't want to include Mike in her deliberations. She had spent so many years in his shadow that it was a deeply imbedded habit and she didn't trust herself to make decisions alone when he was in on the discussion. It hadn't been easy to separate her thoughts from his controlling influence and she found that she often evolved in her thoughts to consider what Mike would do and try to gravitate in that direction.

It was almost beyond her to realize that so many people down through history had actually been able to act independently of outside influence. She felt like she had never had a thought of her own and wouldn't know an original idea if it smacked her in the face.

It was tempting to let go of her new found reality and settle back into her "normal" routine. She was fifty-eight now and not at all practiced in self-discovery. She wondered if it was so important after all.

She laughed at the notion she would forget what she had discovered. She knew she was testing herself to see if she was really committed to exploring her own" reason for being" and she knew that she would never be able to stop now that she was on that course.

Mike had decided to go to Boston while she was in Portland Valley. They had had a long discussion about him going. He had made up his mind to go with her after they had had their long morning's walk. He didn't quite understand yet, that she was not trying to change him. She was trying to change herself.

She was looking forward to going to the reunion by herself and seeing her old friends. This would be an opportunity to try her wings alone and see how good she was at making decisions all by herself. Mike was a trifle concerned, but Boots was so different now that he didn't know how to handle her. He understood some of the process she was going through, but he was still working on his own agenda and needs. However, some strides were being made on both fronts. He had the feeling that he had not only lost control of his marriage, but that Boots was not at all who he had always thought she was. He was intrigued with this new person and spent a fair amount of time trying to figure out how to handle their relationship as it was evolving. Sometimes he felt like it was a good thing he was retiring. He would need all his time just to keep up with this new situation.

He knew he did not want to lose Boots, ever, so he was trying to stay afloat and learn fast. How could she have learned so much so fast?

CHAPTER FORTY THREE

"If the CD salesman comes while I'm gone, have him leave twenty of the new Philadelphia Orchestra disks of Beethoven."

Maxi was getting the store in shape for her time away at the reunion. It seemed that everything was piling up and she would never get it organized. There was coffee to decide on and order and her accountant had not finished this month's payroll. She needed to find a new cleaning service as there was dust on all the book shelves and to top it all off, she had gotten a call yesterday from an attorney representing an international company who wanted to buy her business and turn it into a franchise. She had no idea how to handle that matter, but she was certainly going to check with her lawyer as soon as she got back from Portland Valley. It was giving her much food for thought and the idea of selling her business for enough profit to retire on was very comforting.

She had had prints made of the pictures she had found of the group in high school. There was an especially good one of the five of them standing beside her old Chevy. They were so funny in their long ponytails or short "Pixie" cuts. When she looked at those pictures now and saw how they had dressed and looked, she could remember how much time and effort it took to get them to look like that. She could distinctly remember that they had looked absolutely gorgeous. They must have looked like every other kid in America!

She looked at what she had on now and it was a longish skirt and top and sandals and her hair was short and gray. She went to the mirror and stood there looking at herself trying to see herself as others must see her. She looked like any older woman, same face, same smile, same wrinkles and same clothes.

Maxi had always been a non-conformist in a conformist world and her attitudes and lifestyle had reflected that. Her march had found people who were also non-conformists, but they conformed to each other in like kind and found their own reality and lifestyle.

Her life now encompassed the entire community in which she lived. She was comfortable in the business world she dealt with every day and her life in her church was conformed to the traditions of that church. Her family was in traditional jobs and lived conventional lives.

They were each concerned with the decline of life and the condition of government and the takeover of greed in the society at large, but they were still a part of the world in which they lived. Maxi had evolved into a conventional life, but she knew that she had not compromised herself for any gain. Hers was a life free of the guilt that comes with living selflessly. She really was an honest person and knew that she would have not changed a minute of her life.

She would have the picture of the five friends and the old car reprinted and framed for the reunion. Any other pictures of other classmates, she would bring to the dinner to pass around for everyone to see. There was only a week to go before she was to leave for the trip back to Portland Valley so she would have to hustle to get everything done.

CHAPTER FORTY FOUR

Mary Grace was on the phone talking to the cameraman who was coming to the reunion with her. They were checking his list of equipment and she needed to give him the scenario of what she wanted.

The cameraman was to shoot the film and she had a crewmember acting as director who was to film with a view to setting the finished product into an entertaining momento for the classmates. She would try to shoot as much of the program as possible and use it, out of sequence, to highlight each attendee. She couldn't wait to get to Portland Valley to start filming the exterior shots that would be used to set up and close the film. She already had an idea of what she wanted for these shots and was anxious to get there to see if her memory had served her well and if she had remembered her hometown accurately. She would bring her tape recorder to interview the classmates and other people in the town. She needed to see if her idea to make a film of the effects of small town life had any validity.

Everything was set to go. She had her plane tickets and reservations for a rental car and motel rooms for the two-crew members. They would be on an expense account as she would be able to charge most of the trip to her company.

Hopefully, the film she expected to make with her findings would prove commercially acceptable.

She had lined up a Psychologist and an Anthropologist to help her define the material from her interviews and to weed out or explore further any information she may bring to them in her tapes. The film would be universal in appeal and perhaps, find a wide market. The project interested her enormously.

As she picked up the phone to call Lila, she went over her list for a final time. When Lila answered the phone, she was able to go over with her what she had in mind for the film.

Lila would have invaluable input and Mary Grace was considering asking her to act as director on the final project. She had mentioned the possibility and Lila had been considering it. She laughed when she and Mary Grace were finished with their conversation. Mary Grace asked what was so funny and Lila said there was no way she could not work on her mother's project. She already felt a part of it and wouldn't ever be able to let anyone else direct it. She offered to be in on the early stages and act as coordinator of the script.

Mary Grace breathed a sigh of relief. She had hoped that Lila would become enmeshed in the project and not be able to let it go and that was what had happened. She knew that there was no one better in the business than her daughter.

That settled, they said good-bye and Mary Grace finished packing. She drove her car to the airport and parked in the long-term lot. She would be gone at least a week and if she needed to stay longer to get all the information she needed, she would change her tickets. Her mind was racing with all the possibilities as she hurried into the airport. This was going to be very good!

CHAPTER FORTY FIVE

Nancy sat on the back porch drinking coffee and thinking over the last minute things she wanted to get done for her guests. She and Jean had worked until nine last night finishing the house. They had put up the new curtains that Jean had made. All the bathrooms were turned out in sparkling new linen. Nancy had brought flowers in from the yard and they were in every room in the house. She had loaded the refrigerator with breakfast and lunch foods and had several bottles of wine chilling.

The addition of riding lessons to her schedule had kept her hopping for the past month and she was tired but happy.

Riding had not only given her a sense of accomplishment; it had done wonders for her health. Her muscle tone had improved dramatically after the initial muscle soreness. Her complexion had a healthy glow and her walking stride had improved. She stood upright and looked straight ahead with purpose and determination. She had not been angry with Adam in weeks and frankly, had not thought about him very much. She was beginning to see that he had been a decent husband and father and that he owed her absolutely nothing. She actually felt relieved when she had reached that conclusion. She had never considered that rage and bitterness could be such a burden and that having a say in your own destiny was very freeing.

She finished her coffee and went in to get changed for her riding lesson. She had bought a pair of breeches and boots and a helmet and she had laughed when she put the outfit on. She certainly didn't look like she had when she was fourteen but it wasn't bad. She was pleased.

Her lesson was in the outdoor arena and there were puddles as big as lakes. Maris did not want to ride through them, but Nancy led her into the first puddle and kept her on the track she wanted. After the initial defiance, the mare settled into Nancy's directions. She was an easy horse to get used to and even though she needed encouragement to go faster than a trot, she was getting used to Nancy's handling of her.

Today they would begin to canter. She had been jumping over low crossbars for the past two weeks now and was ready to speed up and advance.

She had begun to consider the possibilities of becoming an instructor in the not too distant future. She knew that the stable needed qualified people to teach the beginners and she had mentioned to Pam that she might want to train for that possibility. Pam had encouraged her and they were going to start evaluating her to see if she was good enough to teach. She felt she was and she was pretty sure she could convince the staff at the stable of her abilities. For now though, she was happy just to be riding Maris around the arena, trotting and coasting over the crossbars.

CHAPTER FORTY SIX

Adam sat at his desk going over his monthly bills. He felt a sense of loss and sadness, of something irretrievable going away from him. He had had this growing feeling for several weeks now and he didn't know where it was coming from.

He had talked to Jean this morning and in the course of the conversation, she had told him about her mother's riding lessons.

Adam was mystified at all the changes in his ex-wife. He had never known her to be anything but dependent and needy. When he had finally worked up the courage to walk out on her, in essence, he had declared her dead. She was not to be a factor in his life and he would live his own life without any further consideration of her as a person.

He had thought that the divorce from Nancy had been final when all the legal work had been completed. He was beginning to realize that the divorce was just now becoming final. More than twenty-five years of living with Nancy had bound them together in a relationship that had been dependent on both sides. Even after the divorce, as long as Nancy ranted and raved about him, he was tied into the relationship. He was sure he had done the right thing and all his friends and family agreed with him. But he was still, somehow, bound up with Nancy.

Now, though, Nancy had moved beyond her anger and she was becoming less and less needy. She seemed to have broken away from that person she had been and found a whole new life.

Essentially Adam had not changed since the divorce. He had kept busy with his agency, dating, and taking trips.

However, that which had sustained him all his life, still sustained him. He liked being in a position of taking care of someone. The women he dated now considered him an ideal date. He was courteous and kind and masculine. They never needed to make plans as Adam always took charge. He was very good at planning an outing and preferred to do so. Women seemed to like him to make the plans.

He had narrowly escaped marriage several times.

But now, he was beginning to feel truly divorced from Nancy Lynn in a spiritual sense. The legal divorce had never had the impact that Adam had thought it would. This new feeling was very different and Adam was trying to deal with the new reality. He felt somehow cheated that she should be able to find herself at the age of fifty eight and come into her own whereas he seemed to be stuck with all their years together as the glue that had held <u>him</u> together.

He wondered for the first time, if there would have been a chance for them to find a life together if he had not walked out.

He realized that it had been cruel and high-handed to walk out on her, but he felt he had acted in self-defense. It had seemed that life was never going to happen to him as long as he had to deal with his wife, and so he had left her. The fact that even her parents understood why he had left her lent credence to the act and he had always felt justified in his actions.

But he still remembered how frightened Nancy had always been. He had not helped her to work through her fears nor encouraged her to move on. He had done what she seemed to want and taken care of her. It had never occurred to him that Nancy's fears were something to overcome that they were shadows that caused a darkness in her life.

He had always been afraid to anger her parents. He was in awe of their money and position and after they had turned the agency over to him, his whole livelihood was tied into them. He needed money to run his household and to raise the kids.

They had all gone to college and had turned out well so he did not regret that he had worked hard at the agency.

He could see now, though, that he was motivated to treat Nancy the way he did, not out of love, but out of fear of disapproval from his in-laws and the income they were providing.

The settlement of the agency to Adam had not been a gift. His father-in-law kept an eye on the business from Florida and the terms included a large income to them out of the profits. He had maintained the legal right to the books and had his accountant go over them every quarter.

The agency would never belong totally to Adam, as Nancy Lynn was a partner in the business. Adam would have to buy her out to own everything, and with the divorce settlement, he would never be able to do that. He had agreed on a generous property settlement and alimony payments as part of the divorce.

Even though her parents realized that the marriage was no good, they would have never left their only daughter high and dry. She had been well provided for by both her parents and Adam. She and her children were their sole heirs when they died and she stood to inherit substantially from them. Her house was a part of the settlement and it was free and clear.

CHAPTER FORTY SEVEN

Adam thought about how young they had been when they married. He had wanted to be the perfect husband and father and had read all the books on the subject. Unfortunately, the books only told him what some mythical ideal was, not how to deal with a wife who was non-functional and in-laws who held the purse strings, not to mention a baby the first year of the marriage.

His generation of men had been smack in the middle of a change that many had not embraced, reasonably sure that the changes were a phase (as radio people had considered television in the early days).

Now, men and women were emerging from the fall-out and realizing that some had lost and some had won and they weren't always who they were supposed to be according to conventional wisdom.

Adam closed the checkbook and took out a piece of paper. He needed to write some of this down and try to make sense of it. He felt as if life were leaving him behind and he wasn't sure he even had a reason to be anymore.

CHAPTER FORTY EIGHT

Sally had arrived at the airport that morning and Jean had picked her up. Nancy Lynn was at home awaiting the arrival of Mary Grace who was driving her rental car in from the airport. Maxi and Boots had gotten in last night. By the time Jean dropped Sally off, everybody was there.

There was much hugging and kissing and exclamations of" God! You haven't changed a bit! "Went round the room in a chorus. They all laughed at each others sweet lying, and they loved it.

It was a beautiful late spring day and Nancy's back porch with the comfortable chairs made an ideal place to sit and get used to each other again. The fact that it was Nancy's house seemed appropriate since they had spent more time in her house when they were in high school than anywhere else. By the time they had each given the bare bones of their lives since high school, they were relaxed and getting comfortable.

There was much to talk about but Nancy interrupted to keep them on track. They needed to plan a menu for their dinner that evening and they needed to shop for the makings. Mary Grace took charge of menu planning and volunteered to do the entree. Nancy Lynn admitted that she could barely boil water and volunteered to get the wine. Boots took on dessert and Maxi; vegetarian still, volunteered to do grilled vegetables. Sally would do salad and rolls.

They all piled into Mary Grace's rental car and at Nancy Lynn's direction, found a decent meat market and produce stand. The season for fresh asparagus and strawberries was upon them and they shopped for the rest of the menu items and went back to Nancy's house.

By the time they got back to Nancy's house, they were ready to cook. Nancy's kitchen was large and well equipped. Adam had designed it, as he had loved to cook and had prepared many of the family's meals over the years. There was plenty of room for everybody to have space to work on their individual offering. Nancy Lynn poured glasses of wine for everybody and they set to work. As the chicken sautéed in a bit of butter, Maxi cleaned and prepped the vegetables. She had asparagus and eggplant and new potatoes. The asparagus and eggplant would be set to marinate in a vinaigrette and grilled just before everything else was ready. The potatoes would be steamed and dressed with sweet butter and parsley. Mary Grace poached the browned chicken in white wine and then reduced the wine until it was almost gone. She added cream and tarragon and reduced that until it was thickened. The wonderful aromas that began to fill the kitchen made them very glad to be exactly where they were.

Sally cleaned lettuce and cucumbers and fresh radishes. She made a simple garlic, olive oil and vinegar dressing to add later and set to work cleaning up after every body else. Her catering expertise was coming in handy.

Boots sliced strawberries and poured raspberry liquor over them. She made a sponge cake and whipped cream. Later she would put everything together in a trifle bowl to serve in dessert dishes.

The longer they worked and the more wine they drank, the more they laughed. They tried to make a guess as to the caloric content of the meal and found it hysterical that each had been on a lifelong, continuous diet. Their stories matched to a "T" as to what they had done to keep from gaining weight. They had been through all the fad diets of the seventies and eighties. They had all tried the liquid hospital diets and they were all now into healthy, fat free diets and lots of exercise.

Maxi was the only one who had always been a vegetarian but she too, had had to battle the "pig demon" and had her own versions of the various diets.

As everything approached readiness, Nancy Lynn set the table with her beautiful china and silver. They sat down to salad at eight and finally served the dessert at 10. There was so much to talk about and so much to discover about each other. The wine and the good food had bonded them again and they were older, wiser versions of their teenage selves. They still had much in common and they found that they still liked each other as much as they had in high school.

Nancy made coffee and the others cleaned up. They went back to the back porch with the coffee and settled in. The caffeine and the joy of being back together again kept them awake. They talked as a group and broke off into groups of two or three and then back together. It was easy to talk about their lives, their common experiences and their unique experiences.

They talked about their children and Nancy told of how she had never really been there for her children. She had never considered her remoteness from her family before and when she listened to her friends talk about their children, she felt empty and stupid. She didn't want to think about what she had lost by her inability to love her family. There was no way to go back now and she knew she would always regret that she had no loving relationship with her two children in California. Jean had stood by her and they were able to communicate more and more as time went by. She loved her two grandsons and they loved her, so all was not lost.

As the evening progressed into night, they listened to each other's stories.

Sally talked about the deaths of Clarence and her two children, and there in that soft June night, he told her friends how she had nearly died herself from the pain of their loss. Maxi went to sit next to her and embraced her when she cried. Each of the friends shuddered to think that what each had feared most as parents had actually happened to Sally. They were absolutely silent in the face of her tragedy and could only offer words of sympathy.

Maxi told her that she could not possibly know how awful it must have been for her. She was grateful that Sally had been able to come back from her loss and make a life for herself. Each of them admitted that they had all had a horror of losing their children before they themselves died. They had all wondered how they would have dealt with it and were glad that at least, their respective children had had the chance to grow into adulthood.

They moved on from that conversation to other areas. Each had their own unique slant on things and told tales ranging from raising children in a commune to eating really strange foods in China. Each of them had a different story on the effects that men had had on their lives.

Mary Grace regretted that she had never been married more than two years to both of her husbands and Maxi felt that never marrying worked quite well for her. Boots described briefly what her marriage to Mike had been like and about her decision to take hold of her own life at this late date. They laughed with Nancy over Adam's interest in her now that she had begun to make a life for herself.

Sally was the most content in her marriage, but then Sally had always been the most able in relationships. Something about her personality or upbringing had schooled her in dealing with people on a personal level. She seemed to suffer much less at the hands of others than most people did.

They were interested and interesting. There were forty years to catch up on not so much because they had once been friends but because they still genuinely liked each other. Finally, all the wine was gone and they were becoming numb with tiredness and drifted off to bed. Tomorrow would be a busy day too, with the rehearsal and each of the friends had people to see in town.

They were having lunch after the rehearsal with several people from the class already in town. Margaret had arranged the luncheon and it would be interesting, as they would be seeing other people they hadn't seen in forty years.

CHAPTER FORTY NINE

There were one hundred and ten classmates at the reunion and many had brought spouses or dates. Nobody could figure out who anybody was except for the people who had always lived in Portland Valley or who had kept up with each other over the years. Nancy Lynn knew more than any of the other friends since she had lived in town all her life and had worked on the committee. She was able to keep most everybody sorted out and after the rehearsal yesterday, names and faces were fitting each other. Name tags with pictures from the yearbook helped as did contact lens and glasses.

It was amazing to Mary Grace that she could remember anybody, but memories were triggered by other's recollections. She had forgotten how they used to pile into cars and head for the drive-in movie. They would hide two people in the trunks of the cars so those two people didn't have to pay and divvy up the savings later at the hamburger joint where they all hung out.

They had all had their first taste of alcohol in high school and Mary Grace remembered one new year's eve party flush with cheap wine, Juicy Fruit gum and cigarettes.

She laughed with the others at how much effort they expended to get ready for a party like that and how little time it must have taken to undo all the bathing, primping and dressing.

Everybody was into the spirit of the event and the skits were very entertaining. Everybody participated and was gratified when their classmates laughed at their lines.

Mary Grace's camera crew added a touch of drama to the evening and all were looking forward to receiving their copy of the tape. After all was said and done, it was a very satisfying reunion. Plans were made for another in five years and Glenn and Margaret made sure to get names on a list.

CHAPTER FIFTY

Sally stayed in Portland Valley until Tuesday and visited her relatives. Mary Grace stayed long enough to scout the town for locations for her movie. She had decided to interview her friends for the basis of her film and they had all agreed to participate. They were even willing to be interviewed on camera and Mary Grace was beginning to see the possibilities of her entire film being based on the very diverse lives of herself and her friends.

Maxi left for New Mexico the day after the reunion to get back and deal with the bookstore. She and Sally made plans to meet in Chicago in August when Maxi was to attend a conference. Boots left, also, on Sunday to get back home and deal with her life.

Mike would already be back from Boston and would meet her at the airport. They were to go out to dinner and Boots was sure that he would be full of information about his trip to Boston. As she boarded the plane, she began to dread going back. There would be Mike, all eager to listen to her and tell her about his trip to Boston.

She had always wanted him to be there for her and now he seemed to be. However, she knew that he would do whatever was necessary to keep his marriage together and his actions smacked more of self-interest than real caring for her. She really didn't want to be patronized. That was just another side of his controlling influence of the past.

It was becoming more and more difficult to believe that Mike could understand where she was going. It was a very bleak feeling as she approached her future and realized that changes would have to be made that would be wrenching. She couldn't go back now and she was not sure how to go ahead.

She was beginning to realize, though, that she had never loved Mike and never would.

Nancy Lynn was happy to have Sally for the extra few days and took her to the stables when she went for a lesson. She had stopped by the YWCA a week ago to inquire about swimming lessons for herself and had seen a poster asking for volunteers for the day camp to be held in July and August. She had inquired and found that they needed a business manager. She had talked to the camp director to find out what the job entailed and the director was so glad to see an actual volunteer, that she signed her up immediately. She could learn on the job!

Adam had called before the reunion and asked if he could talk with her. They had agreed to meet for lunch Wednesday after she had taken Sally to the airport. She couldn't imagine what he wanted. He had totally distanced himself from her after he had walked out and had only called her about the agency or one of the children. She would have only an hour to meet with him as she had a riding lesson in the afternoon and a meeting at the "Y" after that.

She still had to get the house back together after her guests and Margaret and Glenn were having her to dinner. She knew they were trying to fix her up with a friend of theirs, and she even knew who it was, but she decided she would like to meet him. Her life had changed so dramatically in the past few months, that she was open to all sorts of suggestions. Now when she stood by the window in the bedroom and looked out at the stand of trees, she felt whole. There was a growing confidence in her that erased the fear she had previously lived under. She was very much like a flower that blooms late in fall after other flowers have bloomed and died.

EPILOGUE

In 1994 Maxi completed the sale of her business to the franchise outfit. She had hired Sally's husband as attorney for the sale and he had gotten a whopping price for the business. Maxi had retired on the profits and she and Jake had taken a trip together to Australia. They had always had a high regard for each other and had never been as seriously involved with anyone else as they had been with each other.

He had just submitted his fourteenth book to the publisher and had agreed to help Maxi write a book that she had always wanted to write. She wanted to write about people who get caught up in others expectations for them and never find out who they were. She knew that there were hundreds of books about the same subject, but she felt that as she had a voice, it would be her own voice and she wanted to say what she felt.

The book was actually going pretty well. She found that if she wrote honestly, the writing flowed. If she went beyond honesty into "writing" she stopped dead. It was difficult sometimes to know the difference. There was a lot of rewriting going on.

Nancy Lynn had dropped the Lynn part of her name and let it be known that she wanted to be called Nancy. She had made a trip to California to visit her two children there. She would never be able to erase all the years when she was so distant from them, but they were forgiving and had long since come to terms with their mother's lack of parenting skills.

Adam had called once to see if he and Nancy could try again. He had sounded lonely and a little desperate, but Nancy was not interested. It was if he had never truly existed and she didn't see him at all as a potential for shared time.

After the fortieth reunion of her high school class, she had continued with riding and teaching and had bought a mare to keep at the stable. Her grandsons were becoming very good riders and she was able to teach them a lot. They went on trail rides together and had even gotten Jean and her husband to try.

She had a circle of friends now that included Margaret and Glenn and they had found numerous men for her to try out. She never lacked for an escort for an evening out. She hadn't had the television on in months and the last book she had read was a biography of Winston Churchill.

When Boots came home after the reunion, Mike had been excited about his trip to Boston. He had told her about their son's life there and had begun to realize how closed in he and Boots had become. Once he had allowed himself to think of different ways to approach life, he had begun to see the possibilities. His enthusiasm for Brian's life had made him look at possibilities for his own life. They talked at length as to their options and divorce or separation was mentioned more than once.

95

Boots felt that there was no basis for continuing the marriage and she was afraid of falling under Mike's controlling influence again. It was a constant struggle to maintain her own identity and even though she told herself she stayed with Mike for all the right reasons, she still had trouble moving ahead when confronted with his need of her. It had become almost a power trip for her to realize that he needed her more than she needed him and she tried to fight against those feelings. She could not always see what was honest and what was habit. She knew that she would never be free of Mike until she came to terms with her own fears and needs and she grew tired of the process.

She was beginning to realize that both she and Mike had value and even though the marriage had been less than equitable, she could not disregard it. She couldn't stop being honest at this stage of the game, but there was a lot more being revealed about Mike as she became more realistic with herself. She knew that she would be on a journey of self-discovery as long as she lived and she could deal with that.

Jim and Sally settled into a semi-retirement. He still took an occasional case that interested him and was always available as a consultant. Sally had turned the catering business over to her partner as planned. Her partner had paid for the business and was doing even better than Sally had. She was very proud of him and helped when he became frantic, days before a big party.

Cal and Joan had taken a month long trip to Japan and Jim and Sally took Patrick and Alicia to Aspen to teach them how to ski. Sally never laughed so hard in her life as she did watching Patrick try to stay up on skis. If he had been a normal child, she thought, he should have bruises all over him, but he was totally unscathed. Alicia learned early and was very good, but by the end of the week, Patrick was trying the more difficult slopes with all of them.

They planned to get all the grandchildren together in the summer and take them camping.

Sally alternately shuddered and planned for this event. She was sure she and Jim were too old for such an adventure but Jim was adamant that they could do it.

She was taking classes in fly fishing and Chinese cooking and their dinner parties were an odd mixture of freshly caught trout and steamed dumplings. Jim was encouraging her to take woodworking in the next session.

The reunion film was duly finished and sent off to the classmates. It turned out to be hilarious and people played it over and over for their friends and at parties. Some of the camera angles caught people in juxtaposition, as they had never seen themselves before. It was the most treasured momento from their reunion.

The interviews with her friends were done in their own homes and surroundings. The opening shot was a montage of all the women in their present lives. There was a shot of Sally, frantic in the last minutes before a party. Nancy was trying to get four little girls to stay on their ponies long enough to get once around the ring. Maxi was involved with a negotiator from the franchise outfit and was telling them in no uncertain terms what she expected.

Boots was trying to register for a math class at the local community college and was running into glitch after glitch.

The screen abruptly changed to a shot of Portland Valley with its quiet main street square that hadn't changed much since they had all lived there. The camera panned to the suburbs with their fifties ranch homes and into the side streets of town with the rows of Victorian homes and row upon row of maple trees.

The contrast between the opening shots and the serenity of Portland Valley was very affecting and set the tone for Mary Grace's notion of portraying what happens to people who came of age in the sixties, seventies and eighties. She was beginning to realize that this would be the start of a series of films detailing people evolving from different aspects of American life. She already had two researchers trying to find people who had grown up in inner city neighborhoods during the same time period. Next, she would do ethnic Southern and then California migrant families.

That would be difficult as there were not nearly as many records kept on migratory people as mainstream citizens. She would need to depend in large part, on oral history. She had notified her friends that there was much interest in the first film and to be prepared for a fair amount of attention when it was released. ABC had bought the film and would be airing it in November in prime time. There would be heavy promotion during November sweeps and hopefully enough interest generated to guarantee a market for the series. It was definitely looking good.

She had never set out to do anything in her life. When she had been a kid in Portland Valley, her life was free and easy and there were few expectations for her. She wondered when she had become the sort of person who lived to dissect and portray people and the effect that life had on them. There didn't seem to be any outstanding areas in her life that would have caused her to be so focused on this vocation that had encompassed her life and made her whole. She felt lucky to be in a position to do what she loved doing and intended to keep on doing it until she was no longer able to work.

END

ABOUT THE AUTHOR

Patsy A. Mills was born in Alabama and spent her formative years in Tennessee and Kentucky. That southern indoctrination was the deciding mold for much of her early approach to life and has been a large part of the persons who make up *Forty in the Female Lane*.

Ms. Mills has three daughters and seven grandchildren for which she feels richly blessed. At age sixty-two, she retired after twenty-one years as an insurance agent and spent two years as a full-time student at the CULINARY INSTITUTE OF AMERICA.

After graduation, she has spent time practicing her skills on friends, family and various community and social groups. Most are happy to be test subjects even though some things are, perhaps, a bit too creative!